The Cost of the Ukraine War for Russia

HOWARD J. SHATZ, CLINT REACH

Prepared for the Department of the Air Force
Approved for public release; distribution is unlimited.

RAND PROJECT AIR FORCE

For more information on this publication, visit **www.rand.org/t/RRA2421-1**.

About RAND

The RAND Corporation is a research organization that develops solutions to public policy challenges to help make communities throughout the world safer and more secure, healthier and more prosperous. RAND is nonprofit, nonpartisan, and committed to the public interest. To learn more about RAND, visit www.rand.org.

Research Integrity

Our mission to help improve policy and decisionmaking through research and analysis is enabled through our core values of quality and objectivity and our unwavering commitment to the highest level of integrity and ethical behavior. To help ensure our research and analysis are rigorous, objective, and nonpartisan, we subject our research publications to a robust and exacting quality-assurance process; avoid both the appearance and reality of financial and other conflicts of interest through staff training, project screening, and a policy of mandatory disclosure; and pursue transparency in our research engagements through our commitment to the open publication of our research findings and recommendations, disclosure of the source of funding of published research, and policies to ensure intellectual independence. For more information, visit www.rand.org/about/research-integrity.

RAND's publications do not necessarily reflect the opinions of its research clients and sponsors.

Library of Congress Cataloging-in-Publication Data is available for this publication.

ISBN: 978-1-9774-1268-3

Cover: photo by Alamy; cover design by Rick Penn-Kraus.

Limited Print and Electronic Distribution Rights

About This Report

Russia's invasion of Ukraine in February 2022 has proved costly to the Russian federal budget and the Russian economy. In this report, we estimate the costs to the economy as measured by gross domestic product (GDP), the costs of financial capital destruction in the economy, the costs of military operations, and the replacement cost of equipment and weapons destroyed and exquisite munitions expended. We found that, as of September 2022, the direct military costs of the war might have reached $40 billion or 84 percent of 2021 national defense spending. Of this, operations and compensation amounted to $29 billion, and materiel amounted to $11 billion. Furthermore, GDP losses amounted to about $30 billion from April through June 2022, with annual losses for 2022 likely to be between $103 billion and $160 billion—between 6 percent and 9 percent of 2021 GDP, if not higher. In addition, the country has experienced $289 billion in financial capital destruction as measured by the market value of companies on the Moscow Stock Exchange. Over the long term, even with a stalemated war, Russia's economy and the standard of living of its people are likely to decline. The main factor sustaining Russia's economy is the export revenue it earns from oil and gas sales, particularly oil. Even though the Russian economy is declining because of sanctions and other structural factors, and war operations are proving expensive, we judge these costs to be sustainable for the next several years. We completed the main research for this report at the end of August 2022. Accordingly, we focused our analysis on the costs of the first six months of the war and data available through that date. We have included highly selective updates beyond that period. This report was cleared for public release by the Department of the Air Force on September 13, 2023. To account for this publication delay, we have added a brief postscript summarizing the cost of the war through late summer 2023.

The research reported here was conducted within the Strategy and Doctrine Program of RAND Project AIR FORCE as part of a fiscal year 2022 concept formulation project.

Funding

Funding for this research was made possible through the concept formulation provision of the Department of the Air Force–RAND Sponsoring Agreement. PAF uses concept formulation funding to support a variety of activities, including research plan development; direct assistance on short-term, decision-focused Department of the Air Force requests; exploratory research; outreach and communications initiatives; and other efforts undertaken in support of the development, execution, management, and reporting of PAF's approved research agenda.

RAND Project AIR FORCE

RAND Project AIR FORCE (PAF), a division of the RAND Corporation, is the Department of the Air Force's (DAF's) federally funded research and development center for studies and analyses, supporting both the United States Air Force and the United States Space Force. PAF provides the DAF with independent analyses of policy alternatives affecting the development, employment, combat readiness, and support of current and future air, space, and cyber forces. Research is conducted in four programs: Strategy and Doctrine; Force Modernization and Employment; Resource Management; and Workforce, Development, and Health. The research reported here was prepared under contract FA7014-22-D-0001.

Additional information about PAF is available on our website: www.rand.org/paf/.

This report documents work originally shared with the DAF on February 24, 2023. The draft report, issued on September 29, 2022, was reviewed by formal peer reviewers and DAF subject-matter experts.

Acknowledgments

We thank Raphael Cohen of RAND for overall guidance on this research. Reviews by William Courtney, King Mallory, and Mark Stalczynski greatly strengthened the manuscript. At RAND, Julienne Ackerman guided the manuscript through the production process, and Elizabeth White provided expert copy editing. All errors of fact and interpretation remain those of the authors.

Summary

Issue

Russia's renewed invasion of Ukraine encompassed a large increase in defense spending; unleashed a global economic maelstrom of elevated energy, food, and fertilizer prices; and sparked a historic economic sanctions campaign by a united West opposed to the invasion. Russia failed to reach its initial military goals and ended up in a protracted war with significant numbers of dead and wounded, depletion of munitions, and destruction of equipment. As the war continues, it is useful to understand the initial economic costs to Russia and the outlook for Russia's economy.

Approach

We estimated the overall cost of the war to Russia's economy and the direct costs of the military campaign; we then considered the potential consequences of the war and Western sanctions for Russia's economic outlook. We focused on data from the first six months of the war (through August 2022) plus highly selective updates to account for the costs of mobilization in September 2022 and further sanctions against Russian oil and oil products. The findings should be considered rough order-of-magnitude estimates because of the difficulty of obtaining reliable data about Russia's economy. We used data from the Bank of Russia and the Ministry of Finance, as well as a variety of other sources that we assessed to be credible. Given the difficulties of assessing the true market value of the ruble, we used the January 2022 exchange rate of 76 rubles to the dollar.

Conclusions

We estimated that as of late summer of 2022, the war had involved direct costs of almost $40 billion, or 84 percent of 2021 national defense spending. Of this, operations and compensation amounted to $29 billion, and materiel amounted to $11 billion. Furthermore, losses in national income in the economy, as measured by GDP, had amounted to about $30 billion, with annual losses for 2022 likely to be between $103 billion and $160 billion, between 6 percent and 9 percent of 2021 GDP, if not higher. As of the end of June, Russia had experienced $289 billion in financial capital destruction as measured by the market value of companies on the Moscow Stock Exchange.

For comparison, in 2021, Russian national defense spending was $47 billion, federal budget revenues were $333 billion, federal budget expenditures were $326 billion, and GDP was $1.776 trillion, all in nominal terms. Regarding costs to Russia, these estimates include both flows (operations and national income) and stocks (materiel and capital destruction). Some of the military costs are likely captured in national income costs, and so we refrain from aggregating them into a single number.

Over the long term with a stalemated war, Russia's economy and the standard of living of its people are likely to decline. The relative level of technology used in the economy is likely to regress as Russian competitors advance. The main factor sustaining Russia as of late summer 2022 is the export revenues it earns from oil and gas sales, particularly oil. Blocking those could be the most powerful tool in the West's economic toolkit to hamper Russia's war effort, but doing so would be politically difficult in a world in which major countries beyond the Western alliance benefit from continued purchases of Russian oil at discounted prices.

Even though the Russian economy is declining because of sanctions and other structural factors, and war operations are proving expensive, we judge these costs to be sustainable for the next several years. War costs alone will not cause Russia to end its Ukraine invasion. More likely, a combination of battlefield losses, economic decline, a drop in living standards, social unrest, and elite dissatisfaction will be among the driving forces behind any potential change in Russia's war effort.

This report was cleared for public release by the Department of the Air Force on September 13, 2023. To account for this publication delay, we have added a brief postscript with updated costs, using the same methods. Using updated data, we estimated that the war caused Russia GDP losses of between $81 billion and $104 billion in 2022. Regarding direct military spending, we estimated that Russia is poised to spend a minimum of $131.6 billion from early 2022 through 2024. The war remains sustainable for Russia from the perspective of costs.

Contents

About This Report iii

Summary v

Figures and Tables viii

Chapter 1. Introduction 1

    Caveats and the Plan for This Report 3

Chapter 2. Overall Costs 5

    Measuring the Economic Consequences 6

    GDP 7

    Capital Destruction 10

    Looking Ahead 14

Chapter 3. Direct Military Costs 15

    Approach 16

    Cost of Long-Range Precision Weapons Expenditure 28

    Conclusion 30

Chapter 4. The Mechanisms of Russian Economic Decline 32

    The Fundamental Problem Facing the Russian Economy 32

    Outperformance of Expected Underperformance 32

    Stresses on the Russian Economy 35

Chapter 5. A Future of Likely Decline 40

    Military Losses and the Challenge of Rebuilding the Russian Armed Forces 40

    Near-Term Ramifications 41

    Long-Term Economic Decline 42

    The Future of the Russian Threat 43

Chapter 6. Postscript: The Costs of War by Late Summer 2023 44

    Overall Costs 45

    Underlying Patterns in the Russian Economy 50

    Direct Military Costs 53

    Conclusion 55

Abbreviations 57

Bibliography 58

Figures and Tables

Figures

Figure 4.1. The Price of Russian Oil Versus the International Benchmark 36
Figure 6.1. Monthly Average of the Daily Ruble-Dollar Exchange Rate 45
Figure 6.2. The Price of Russian Oil Versus the International Benchmark 53
Figure 6.3. The Price Discount for Russian Oil 53

Tables

Table 2.1. Projected Russian GDP Loss, 2022 8
Table 2.2. Percentage Changes in Real GDP, Relative to the Same Period in the
      Previous Year 9
Table 2.3. Market Capitalization of the Moscow Exchange Equities Market............................11
Table 2.4. Capitalization of the Moscow Exchange Aggregate Bond Index (RUABITR) 12
Table 3.1. Cost to Russia of Military Operations..16
Table 3.2. Russian Fixed- and Rotary-Wing Losses in Ukraine War as of
      Mid-September 2022 18
Table 3.3. Selected Russian Ground Forces Systems and Replacements 26
Table 3.4. Selected Russian Ground Losses in Ukraine War, as of September 19, 2022 27
Table 3.5. Russian Missiles Employed in Ukraine...29
Table 3.6. Reported Number of Russian Missiles Employed in Ukraine through August 2022...29
Table 3.7. Estimated Total Direct Military Costs, February 24, 2022, to September 19, 2022....31
Table 4.1. Russia's Goods and Services Trade in Billions of Dollars...33
Table 4.2. The Russian Federal Budget...34
Table 4.3. Changes in the Bank of Russia Key Rate..35
Table 4.4. Industrial Production in 2022 Relative to the Same Month in 2021 38
Table 5.1. Monthly GDP in 2022 Relative to the Same Period in 2021 40
Table 6.1. Projected 2022 GDP Growth Before Russia's Invasion of Ukraine 46
Table 6.2. Revised Projected Russian GDP Loss, 2022...47
Table 6.3. Market Capitalization of the Moscow Exchange Equities Market............................49
Table 6.4. Russia's Goods and Services Trade, Billion U.S. Dollars 51
Table 6.5. Industrial Production Relative to the Same Month in the Previous Year...................52
Table 6.6. Selected Russian Weapons Losses, September 2022 through September 2023 54
Table 6.7. The Minimum Direct Cost of Russia's War on Ukraine, 2022–2024 (trillion rubles).55

Chapter 1. Introduction

Russia's full-scale invasion of Ukraine on February 24, 2022, unleashed a global economic maelstrom of elevated energy, food, and fertilizer prices and a historic economic sanctions campaign by the West. Russia failed to reach its initial, sweeping military goals and ended up in a protracted war with large numbers of dead and wounded, depleted exquisite munitions, and heavy losses of weapons and equipment.

The Western sanctions campaign and the extended war have proved costly for Russia. Already growing slowly because of economic mismanagement and sanctions instituted after its 2014 annexation of Crimea and invasion of eastern Ukraine, the prognosis of many observers was that Russia's growth chances would be damaged even further and that it would regress technologically.[1] Furthermore, the demands of the military campaign turned out to be well beyond what Moscow anticipated, requiring greater military expenditures and further damaging the Russian economy.

For this report, we estimated the cost of the war to Russia. We expect this information will be of interest primarily to policymakers, practitioners, and scholars focusing on Russia's ability to sustain the war effort, but also to researchers focusing on Russia and the security of Europe and to the general public interested in the course of Russia's war against Ukraine. Even though the Russian economy is declining because of sanctions and other structural factors and war operations are proving expensive, we judge these costs to be sustainable for the next several years.

As of late summer 2022, the war itself had been expensive but manageable for Russia, and there is little indication that over the short term the direct costs of the war will drive Russia to halt its aggression or exit Ukraine. But in combination with the costs to the economy of sanctions, other economic factors could affect Russian decisionmaking about continued pursuit of the war.

Based on projected changes in gross domestic product (GDP), we estimated that the sanctions and the war will cost Russia between $103 billion and $160 billion in lost GDP in 2022.[2] This also can be thought of as lost income and equals between 6 percent and 9 percent of 2021 GDP. This is a conservative estimate as it does not account for inflation. Using the actual decline of GDP in April through June 2022, we estimated that the total cost to the economy for those three months was $28 billion to $33 billion. This is a rough estimate based on several

---

[1] John Bryson, "Russia as a Low-Tech Nation—Severing the Country from Global Supply Chains with the Ukrainian War," University of Birmingham, June 17, 2022; Branko Milanovic, "The Novelty of Technologically Regressive Import Substitution," *Global Policy*, May 18, 2022b.

[2] *GDP* is the total value of all goods and services produced in an economy.

strong assumptions. In addition, the value of companies traded on the Moscow Stock Exchange fell by $289 billion through June 30, 2022, a decline of 35 percent.

Beyond the war's consequences for the broader economy, Russia's invasion has also had direct costs. We estimated that Russia's direct military costs through late summer 2022 amount to $40 billion or almost 76 percent of 2021 national defense spending. Of this, operations and compensation amounted to $29 billion, and materiel amounted to $11 billion.

These estimates of the cost to overall economy and the cost of the war include both flows (military operations, compensation, and national income) and stocks (military materiel and capital destruction). Some of the military costs are likely captured in national income costs, and so we refrain from aggregating them into a single number.

For comparison, in 2021, Russian national defense spending was $47 billion, federal budget expenditures were $326 billion, federal budget revenues were $333 billion, and GDP was $1.776 trillion, all in nominal terms.[3] For comparison, U.S. GDP that same year was $23.315 trillion, and that of China was $17.734 trillion; Russia was the 11th largest economy, between number 10 South Korea and number 12 Brazil. As an additional comparison, the $18.2 billion worth of security assistance that the United States has provided to Ukraine between February 24, 2022, and November 4, 2022, amounted to 2.5 percent of the authorized fiscal year 2022 (October 2021 to September 2022) U.S. defense budget.[4] Note that the figure for Russian national defense spending is only the national defense budget chapter in Ministry of Finance data. Additional defense-related spending appears elsewhere in the budget, such as in housing, education, health care, and social policy.[5]

Medium- and long-term estimates of the cost might be different and more negative, perhaps strikingly so. Militarily, a return to the intensity of operations of March and April 2022 might prove financially draining, as could an extended occupation and possible Ukrainian insurgency.

---

[3] GDP is from World Bank, World Development Indicators, online database, last updated July 20, 2022, variable "GDP (current US$) (Billion)," series code NY.GDP.MKTP.CD. Federal defense spending and budget numbers are from Ministry of Finance of the Russian Federation, Federal Budget, spreadsheet, February 11, 2022a. Ruble values are converted at a rate of 76 to the U.S. dollar to be consistent with calculations throughout this report, as explained in this chapter. The actual average annual ruble-dollar exchange rate for 2021 was 73.7, which would make defense spending for 2021 equal to almost $48.6 billion and lower the military costs of the war in 2022 to 72.1 percent of 2021 defense spending. The source for the ruble-dollar exchange rate is Organization for Economic Co-operation and Development, National Currency to US Dollar Exchange Rate: Average of Daily Rates for the Russian Federation [CCUSMA02RUM618N], retrieved from FRED, Federal Reserve Bank of St. Louis, August 2, 2022.

[4] U.S. Department of Defense, "Fact Sheet on U.S. Security Assistance to Ukraine," fact sheet, November 4, 2022; U.S. Senate, Committee on Armed Services, "Summary of the Fiscal Year 2022 National Defense Authorization Act," December 7, 2021. According to the summary, total defense spending, which includes additional defense spending for the Department of Energy and defense-related activities outside the jurisdiction of the National Defense Authorization Act, amounted to an authorization of $777.7 billion, so Ukraine assistance equaled 2.3 percent of this amount.

[5] Julian Cooper, *Russian Military Expenditure: Data, Analysis and Issues*, FOI-R—3688—SE, FOI, Swedish Defense Research Agency, September 2013.

Economically, the country could face a regression comparable with the era of stagnation of the late 1970s and 1980s.

Caveats and the Plan for This Report

Several issues suggest that our estimates are more of a rough orders of magnitude than exact figures.[6] Most important is the issue of missing military and economic data. Since the war started, Russia has been withholding a large amount of information or reporting only aggregate values and offering implausible loss figures.[7] Suppressed data include specific categories of federal budget spending, such as national defense, national security and law enforcement, and social spending to support the population. Suppressed data also include disaggregated foreign trade figures, the publication of which was suspended in April 2022.[8] This includes the volume of oil exports. Even when we used official Russia data, informed observers suggested skepticism of the reliability of virtually any information coming from Russia.[9] Accordingly, any estimate of economic and military costs must be pieced together from sparse available primary sources, secondary sources, and estimation or modeling.[10] At the same time, data from the Bank of Russia (the Russian central bank) and Ministry of Finance, which we relied on for a large portion of the analysis in this report, are used by a variety of Western institutions and researchers in their analysis of the Russian economy. Data publicly generated by these institutions are also of value to countries that support or tolerate Russia's war, so some degree of institutional credibility and data accuracy is likely important to these institutions. Accordingly, we considered this information to be the most reliable. Other open-source data (on military costs, for example) were, in our view, less reliable and subject to greater error; thus, they merit more skepticism by the reader.

---

[6] We have generally refrained from confidence intervals—a range of estimates for which we are relatively certain—because we have very little basis for constructing such a range. Were we to use our expert judgment to construct such a range, it is likely we would be too narrow (this is a bias known as *anchoring in the assessment of subjective probability distributions*, as described in Amos Tversky and Daniel Kahneman, "Judgment Under Uncertainty: Heuristics and Biases," *Science*, New Series, Vol. 185, No. 4157, September 27, 1974, pp. 1124-1131.) Our one exception is in some computations of change in value of GDP because we base those (computations) on data from the Bank of Russia, which gives a range in their projections of GDP change.

[7] Yulia Starostina, "Secret Economy: What Hiding the Stats Does for Russia," Carnegie Endowment for International Peace, July 1, 2022.

[8] "Russia Suspends Publication of Import-Export Data to Avoid 'Speculation'" Reuters, April 21, 2022.

[9] Christopher Bort, "Why the Kremlin Lies: Understanding Its Loose Relationship with the Truth," Carnegie Endowment for International Peace, January 6, 2022.

[10] An example of a comprehensive effort in this direction, though one with a distinct point of view, is Jeffrey A. Sonnenfeld, Steven Tian, Franek Sokolowski, Michal Wyrebkowski, Mateusz Kasprowicz, and Yale Chief Executive Leadership Institute Researchers, *Business Retreats and Sanctions are Crippling the Russian Economy: Measures of Current Economic Activity and Economic Outlook Point to Devastating Impact on Russia*, Yale University, July 2022.

The conversion of rubles, the Russian national currency, into U.S. dollars also presented a challenge. Immediately after the West started sanctions against Russia, the Bank of Russia (the Central Bank of the Russian Federation) instituted a broad variety of defensive measures, including severely limiting trade in the ruble. Were the capital account to be free, there could be large-scale capital flight and the ruble could collapse. So there was no way to assess the true market value of the ruble. Accordingly, we used the ruble-dollar average monthly exchange rate of 76 rubles to the dollar from January 2022, the last full month before the war, to convert all ruble prices to dollars.[11]

This report proceeds as follows. We start with estimates of the overall cost to the economy, then focus on the direct costs of the military campaign, and then return to the overall economy by discussing in a more qualitative fashion the many ways that the economic campaign against Russia and Russia's war effort are degrading Russia's economy. A final chapter provides conclusions. We completed the main research for this report at the end of August 2022. Accordingly, we focus our analysis on the costs of the first six months of the war and data available through that date. We have included highly selective updates beyond that period, such as estimated costs related to mobilization that Russia announced in September 2022 and further sanctions against Russian oil and oil products exports. In addition, we provide GDP changes in constant terms, as is conventionally done, but all other values in nominal terms. Even though inflation during this period was high, the time period is short enough that differences between nominal and constant values should be small and orders of magnitude should be similar.

This report was cleared for public release by the Department of the Air Force on September 13, 2023. To account for this publication delay, we have added a brief postscript summarizing the cost of the war through late summer 2023.

---

[11] The actual value was 75.8682, but we believed rounding to 76 would be adequate. Exchange rates were sourced from Organization for Economic Co-operation and Development, 2022.

Chapter 2. Overall Costs

Western sanctions and economic restrictions against Russia have been the most invasive against any major power in at least the post–World War II era. They have included sanctions on the Bank of Russia and Russia's foreign reserves, on a large number of Russian banks and defense companies, and on Russian leaders and major business figures.[12] Notably, sanctions and economic restrictions included broad new export controls on most technology items, goods that Russia needs not only for its military production but also for civilian production. Nearly all economically advanced countries joined in the sanctions, with more rolling out.[13]

Beyond direct effects, the sanctions and economic restrictions have made it more difficult to conduct international transactions with Russia, and even when allowed, firms and banks have diminished their activities with Russia as a risk-mitigation measure. As of late summer 2022, a notable exception to Western sanctions was that Russia's global oil and gas exports, a major source of Russian revenue, were not blocked. In addition, the sanctions did not block trade in fertilizer, agricultural products, or medicine.[14]

---

[12] U.S. Department of the Treasury, "U.S. Treasury Announces Unprecedented and Expansive Sanctions Against Russia, Imposing Swift and Severe Economic Costs," press release, February 24, 2022a; U.S. Department of the Treasury, "U.S. Treasury Imposes Sanctions on Russian Federation President Vladimir Putin and Minister of Foreign Affairs Sergei Lavrov," press release, February 25, 2022b; U.S. Department of the Treasury, "Treasury Prohibits Transactions with Central Bank of Russia and Imposes Sanctions on Key Sources of Russia's Wealth," press release, February 28, 2022c; U.S. Department of the Treasury, "Treasury Sanctions Russians Bankrolling Putin and Russia-Backed Influence Actors," press release, March 3, 2022d; U.S. Department of the Treasury, "Treasury Sanctions Kremlin Elites, Leaders, Oligarchs, and Family for Enabling Putin's War Against Ukraine," press release, March 11, 2022e; U.S. Department of Commerce, "Commerce Implements Sweeping Restrictions on Exports to Russia in Response to Further Invasion of Ukraine," press release, February 24, 2022; European Council and Council of the European Union, "Timeline—EU Restrictive Measures Against Russia over Ukraine," webpage, last reviewed on September 14, 2022; United Kingdom Foreign Commonwealth and Development Office, "UK Sanctions Following Russia's Invasion of Ukraine," webpage, last updated July 26, 2022.

[13] Following the full invasion on February 24, 2022, and as of August 30, 2022, the following countries and jurisdictions had placed sanctions on Russia: Australia, Canada, the European Union (the 27 members collectively and some members individually), the G-7 advanced industrial economies as a group (Canada, France, Germany, Italy, Japan, the United States, and the United Kingdom), Japan, New Zealand, Singapore, South Korea, Switzerland, Taiwan, the United Kingdom, and the United States (Richard Martin, "Sanctions Against Russia—A Timeline," S&P Global, webpage, December 21, 2022).

[14] U.S. Department of the Treasury, "Treasury Releases Fact Sheet on Food and Fertilizer-Related Authorizations Under Russia Sanctions; Expands General License Authorizing Agricultural Transactions," press release, July 14, 2022f; Delegation of the European Union to the Holy See, Order of Malta, United Nations Organisations in Rome and to the Republic of San Marino, "EU Sanctions Do Not Restrict EU and Third Countries' Trade in Agrifood Products," press release, June 24, 2022.

Measuring the Economic Consequences

Sanctions and distortions caused by channeling government spending toward the military effort have had consequences for Russia through a multiplicity of channels. Identifying these channels and tallying the costs bottom-up would be one way to estimate an overall cost, but this carries the risk of missing some important costs. With a population of 142.3 million, nominal GDP of $1.776 trillion, and 2.64 million business enterprises in 2021, the economy of Russia is complex, and accounting for all the consequences on each of the economic units and households in Russia would be difficult.[15] Even focusing on major enterprises could leave out the collectively large effects on smaller enterprises. Instead, all these costs can be aggregated into consequences for GDP. This provides estimates of three equivalent economic variables: total expenditures on final goods and services, total incomes earned in an economy (including profits), and total value added along the production chain.[16] Accordingly, changes in GDP reflect the total cost (or benefit) of an event. We considered actual and projected changes in GDP to arrive at an overall cost measure.

Considering changes in GDP will not include the entire cost, as it will not include the cost of destruction of capital. Destruction of physical capital in Russia has been too small to be consequential in measures of costs of the war. But destruction of financial capital can be measured. To do so, we considered the total change in the capitalization of equities listed on the Moscow Stock Exchange and the capitalization of the Moscow Exchange aggregate bond index.

The war will likely have a variety of longer-term costs, which we did not describe. For example, potentially about $300 billion in Russian reserves are frozen under sanctions, and they might ultimately be confiscated to pay for reconstruction in Ukraine. Likewise, Russia might see permanent decreases in oil and gas sales as Europe—which, until the war, was the primary purchaser of both—finds other suppliers and Russia has trouble redirecting sales to other countries that match the full amount previously sold to Europe. Furthermore, Russia might, over a long period, pay a higher rate of interest on sovereign debt to account for the increased risk of dealing with a country that threatens or invades its neighbors. These costs are both beyond the period under consideration in this report and are highly uncertain, but they might manifest throughout the decade of the 2020s.

---

[15] Population data are from United States Census Bureau, International Database, online database, last revised December 21, 2021. Business enterprises are from Statista Research Department, Number of Active Business Enterprises in Russia from 2017 to 2021 (in Millions), database, October 10, 2022b.

[16] Stephanie H. McCulla and Shelly Smith, *Measuring the Economy: A Primer on GDP and the National Income and Product Accounts*, Bureau of Economic Analysis, U.S. Department of Commerce, December 2015.

GDP

In 2021, Russia had largely recovered from the coronavirus disease 2019 (COVID-19)–induced shutdowns and recession of 2020. In real U.S. dollar terms, Russian GDP was $1.46 trillion in 2019, $1.42 trillion in 2020, and $1.49 trillion in 2021.[17] Furthermore, the outlook for 2022 was positive. On February 11, 2022, the Bank of Russia projected that GDP would grow between 2 percent and 3 percent in 2022, between 1.5 percent and 2.5 percent in 2023, and between 2 percent and 3 percent in 2024.[18] That same day, the bank raised its key interest rate from 8.5 percent to 9.5 percent because of rising inflation induced by the rapid economic recovery.

Cost of the War Using Annual GDP Projections

The Russian invasion of Ukraine destroyed those projections. The Bank of Russia changed its 2022 GDP projection to a decrease of between 8 percent and 10 percent.[19] For 2023, it changed its projection to between 0 and –3 percent. However, for a variety of reasons (discussed in Chapter 4), Russia's economy did not perform as poorly as expected. In July 2022, the Bank of Russia changed its projections once again to a decline of between 4 percent and 6 percent in 2022, a decline of 1 percent and 4 percent in 2023, and an increase of between 1.5 percent and 2.5 percent in 2024.[20] Note that Russia was not alone in revising its projections upward. In April 2022, the International Monetary Fund projected that Russian GDP would decline by 8.5 percent in 2022 and 2.3 percent in 2023.[21] But by July 2022, it projected that Russian GDP would decline by only 6.0 percent in 2022 and by 3.5 percent in 2023.[22] We used the July estimates from the Bank of Russia for our main calculations of cost.[23]

---

[17] World Bank, 2022b. The specific variable is GDP (constant 2015 US$) (Billion), series code NY.GDP.MKTP.KD.

[18] Bank of Russia, "The Bank of Russia Increases the Key Rate by 100 b.p. to 9.50% p.a.," press release, February 11, 2022a.

[19] Bank of Russia, "Statement by Bank of Russia Governor Elvira Nabiullina in Follow-Up to Board of Directors Meeting on 29 April 2022," April 29, 2022h.

[20] Bank of Russia "Bank of Russia's Medium-Term Forecast Following the Bank of Russia Board of Directors' Key Rate Meeting on 22 July 2022," press release, July 22, 2022n.

[21] International Monetary Fund, *World Economic Outlook Update: War Sets Back the Global Recovery*, April 2022b.

[22] International Monetary Fund, *World Economic Outlook Update: Gloomy and More Uncertain*, July 2022c.

[23] In a subsequent projection, released October 28, 2022, the Bank of Russia further moderated its projected GDP change for 2022 to a decline of between 3 percent and 3.5 percent but left the forecast for 2023 the same as in July, expecting a decline of between 4 percent and 1 percent. Likewise, it moderated its projection of fourth-quarter 2022 GDP relative to fourth-quarter 2021 GDP—projecting in October a decline within the range of 6.4 percent to 7.8 percent, as compared with the July projection of between 8.5 percent and 12 percent. However, it projected a worse performance of fourth-quarter 2023 GDP relative to fourth-quarter 2022 GDP—projecting in October an increase of between 0 percent and 1.5 percent but projecting in July an increase of between 1 percent and 2.5 percent (Bank of Russia, *October 2022 Monetary Policy Report*, No. 4, November 8, 2022s).

Based on these figures, we estimated that the invasion of and war in Ukraine is expected to cost the Russian economy between $103 billion and $160 billion in lost GDP in 2022, which also can be thought of as lost income (Table 2.1). This is a lower-bound estimated range because it does not take account of inflation in Russia. Year-over-year inflation in Russia was 9.4 percent in February (the month Russia invaded), hit 17.1 percent in March, and then 17.8 percent, 17.1 percent, and 15.9 percent in April, May, and June, respectively.[24] In its July 2022 forecast, the Bank of Russia projected year-on-year inflation for 2022 to range between 13.8 percent and 14.7 percent.[25] Taking account of inflation suggests that losses could range between $117 billion and $184 billion in 2022 dollars.

Table 2.1. Projected Russian GDP Loss, 2022

Project Description	Low	High
2022 GDP change, Bank of Russia January projection (%)	2.0	3.0
2022 GDP change, Bank of Russia July projection (%)	−4.0	−6.0
Total projected change from prewar projections (%)	−6.0	−9.0
Lost GDP		
U.S. dollar terms (billion)	107	160
Ruble terms (billion)	7,848	11,772
U.S. dollar terms with ruble terms converted at 76 rubles/dollar (billion)	103	155
Addendum: 2021 Nominal Russian GDP		
U.S. dollars (billion)	1,775.8	
Russian rubles (billion)	130,795.3	

SOURCES: Bank of Russia, "Bank of Russia's Medium-Term Forecast Following the Bank of Russia Board of Directors' Key Rate Meeting on 11 February 2022," press release, February 11, 2022b; Bank of Russia, 2022n; World Bank, 2022b.
NOTE: Projected GDP changes are in real terms, whereas lost GDP is in nominal terms and therefore assumes zero inflation. Russia has experienced high inflation since the invasion. Accordingly, these figures are a lower-bound range of estimates, and the loss is potentially 10 percent to 20 percent higher in real terms. The U.S. dollar estimate for lost GDP uses the dollar figure for 2021 nominal GDP from the World Bank's World Development Indicators. The ruble estimate uses the ruble figure for 2021 nominal GDP from the same source. The second estimate in U.S. dollar terms converts ruble losses at the rate of 76 rubles to the dollar (as explained in Chapter 1).

Cost of the War Using Actual and Projected Quarterly GDP Losses

Russia reports GDP changes quarterly relative to GDP in the same quarter the previous year. Here we used the reported change in GDP in the second quarter of 2022 to calculate losses because of the war. Regrettably, it was not clear from the announcement whether the change is

---

[24] Bank of Russia, *Regional Economy: Commentaries by Bank of Russia Main Branches*, No. 11, April 2022d; Bank of Russia, *Regional Economy: Commentaries by Bank of Russia Main Branches*, No. 13, July 2022k.

[25] Bank of Russia, 2022n.

based on seasonally adjusted quarterly GDP, so valid comparisons with the previous quarter could not be calculated easily.

Russia reported a real GDP decline of 4 percent in the second quarter of 2022 relative to the second quarter of 2021 (Table 2.2). GDP in the second quarter of 2021 measured 30.9149 trillion rubles in current prices.[26] Year-on-year inflation for June 2022 was 15.9 percent, making second quarter 2021 GDP equivalent to 35.8304 trillion rubles in second quarter 2022 prices.[27] Assuming a 2-percent to 3-percent quarterly growth rate in the absence of the war, and a 4-percent decline because of the war (year-on-year), a rough estimate of the loss caused by the war is between 2.1498 trillion rubles and 2.5081 trillion rubles for the second quarter, or between $28.3 billion and $33.0 billion at an exchange rate of 76 rubles to the dollar. Annualized, this would equal $113 billion to $132 billion overlapping with the lower end of the range of estimates stemming from the use of annual projections, described above.[28]

Table 2.2. Percentage Changes in Real GDP, Relative to the Same Period in the Previous Year

Year	First Quarter	Second Quarter	Third Quarter	Fourth Quarter	Full Year
2021	−0.3	10.5	4.0	5.0	4.7
2022	3.5	−4.0			

SOURCES: Federal State Statistical Service (Rosstat), "Second GDP Estimate 2021 [Вторая оценка ВВП за 2021 год]," Moscow, April 8, 2022a; Federal State Statistical Service (Rosstat), "Rosstat Presents the First Estimate of GDP for the 1st Quarter [Росстат представляет первую оценку ВВП за I квартал 2022года]," Moscow, June 17, 2022b; Federal State Statistical Service (Rosstat), "On a Preliminary Estimate of GDP Dynamics in the II Quarter of 2022 [О предварительной оценке динамики ВВП во II квартале 2022 года]," Moscow, August 12, 2022d.

The annualized estimate based on the decline in second-quarter GDP likely is low. The Russian Central Bank forecasted fourth-quarter 2022 GDP to be between 8.5 percent and 12 percent lower than fourth-quarter 2021 GDP, and it expected inflation in December 2022 to be between 12 percent and 15 percent relative to December 2021.[29] Nominal GDP in the fourth quarter of 2021 was 38.7833 trillion rubles. GDP would have grown by 2 percent from the fourth quarter of 2021 to the fourth quarter of 2022 in the absence of the war. If GDP falls by 8.5 percent to 12 percent from the fourth quarter of 2021 to the fourth quarter of 2022 instead of

---

[26] Federal State Statistical Service (Rosstat), "GDP Quarters (Since 1995), Gross Domestic Product, National Accounts, Statistics," Excel spreadsheet, August 12, 2022c.

[27] Inflation is from Bank of Russia, 2022k. This calculation presumes that GDP is calculated at end-of-quarter values.

[28] The estimate using quarterly data made several strong assumptions and so is a very rough estimate. The 4-percent decline in GDP was based on real values, likely with an index year of 2016, and a decline in nominal GDP as presented here might be different. In addition, because the quarterly data might not be seasonally adjusted, annualizing the loss could be inaccurate. Accordingly, this figure is best considered to be an order-of-magnitude loss rather than a specific estimate.

[29] Bank of Russia, 2022n.

growing by 2 percent, and if inflation is included, quarterly losses would be estimated to be between $60 billion and $80 billion (or $243 billion to $324 billion on an annualized basis), well above the range of the estimates based on the annual forecast.[30]

Capital Destruction

Although the war has not resulted in much physical destruction within Russia, capital destruction has taken place. One type is the destruction of the value of Russian companies. The other is human capital destruction—the exit of people from Russia.

Financial Capital Destruction

One measure of capital destruction is the change in the total stock market capitalization on the Moscow Exchange, the main stock market in Russia. Total capitalization is the summed value of each publicly traded company. At 8:05 a.m. Moscow time on the morning of February 24, 2022, the exchange suspended trading until further notice, but then announced at 9:40 a.m. that trading would resume at 10:00 a.m.[31] Nonetheless, the stock exchange collapsed, and trading was shut down. In early March 2022, the founder of an investment group in an interview on Russian television declared the stock market dead.[32] Selected trading restarted on March 21, 2022, with normal equity and bond trading restarting on March 28, 2022, though for only a half day.[33]

---

[30] The same methodological caveats apply here as applied to the computations based on second-quarter GDP, with the strongest assumption involving the application of real growth rates to nominal values. Specific assumptions for this calculation were that inflation year-on-year in December 2022 would be 13.5 percent and that GDP would have growth by 2 percent from the fourth quarter of 2021 to the fourth quarter of 2022 in the absence of the war. The calculation was done as follows: (1) Multiply fourth quarter 2021 nominal GDP of 38.7833 trillion rubles by 1.135 to take account of expected inflation, assuming GDP is measured at end-of-year prices, yielding 44.0190 trillion rubles. (2) If GDP were to have grown by 2 percent but instead were to fall by between 8.5 percent and 12 percent, the total loss would be between 10.5 percent and 14 percent, so multiply 44.0190 by 0.895 and by 0.86 to get an estimated range of GDP in the fourth quarter of 2022. These two amounts were 39.3970 trillion and 37.8564 trillion. (3) Then subtract the fourth quarter 2022 estimates from the fourth quarter 2021 actual figure to get the value of the loss in rubles. This ranged from 4.622 trillion to 6.163 trillion. (4) Next, divide these numbers by 76 to get dollar figures: $60.8 billion and $81.1 billion. (5) Finally, multiply those dollar figures by 4 to get annualized totals, $243.3 billion and $324.4 billion.

[31] Moscow Exchange, "Moscow Exchange Has Suspended Trading on All of its Markets Until Further Notice," press release, February 24, 2022a; Moscow Exchange, "Moscow Exchange Resumes Trading on its Markets at 10:00am," press release, February 24, 2022b.

[32] Alexander Butmanov, founder of the investment group Allies (союзники), in the interview on RBC TV first said (in Russian), "Worst case scenario, I'm going to work as a Santa Claus as I did 25 years ago," and then followed up by drinking a toast from a bottle of carbonated water, saying, "Dear stock market, you were close to us, you were interesting, rest in peace dear comrade" (Peter Liakhov [@peterliakhov], "A snapshot of the Russian economy," Twitter post, March 3, 2022).

[33] Dezan Shira & Associates, "Moscow Stock Exchange Resumes Selected Trading," *Russia Briefing*, March 21, 2022; "Moscow Exchange to Resume Shares and Bond Trading in Normal Mode on Monday," Reuters, March 26, 2022.

The value of the Moscow Exchange did indeed collapse (Table 2.3). Total market capitalization rose 22 percent in 2021, with those gains coming steadily in the first three quarters. Then, in the first quarter of 2022—the first quarter in which the war took place—market capitalization fell almost 25 percent, destroying 15.5 trillion rubles worth of value ($205 billion). Total market capitalization fell a further 14 percent in the second quarter of 2022, destroying 6.4 trillion rubles worth of value ($84 billion).[34] It then fell yet again in the third quarter, this time by 17.5 percent, destroying more than 7.1 trillion rubles ($94 billion).

Table 2.3. Market Capitalization of the Moscow Exchange Equities Market

Date	Value in Trillions of Rubles	Value in Billions of Dollars
December 31, 2020	51.43	677
March 31, 2021	56.42	742
June 30, 2021	59.84	787
September 30, 2021	65.05	856
December 31, 2021	62.82	827
March 31, 2022	47.30	622
June 30, 2022	40.89	538
September 30, 2022	33.75	444

SOURCES: Moscow Exchange, "Moscow Exchange Announces Results for the Full Year 2020," press release, March 5, 2021a; Moscow Exchange, "Moscow Exchange Announces Results for the First Quarter of 2021," press release, April 30, 2021b; Moscow Exchange, "Moscow Exchange Announces Results for the Second Quarter of 2021," press release, August 20, 2021c; Moscow Exchange, "Moscow Exchange Announces Results for the Third Quarter of 2021," press release, October 29, 2021d; Moscow Exchange, "Moscow Exchange Announces Results for the Full Year 2021," press release, March 4, 2022c; Moscow Exchange, "Moscow Exchange Announces Results for Q1 2022," press release, April 29, 2022d; Moscow Exchange, "Moscow Exchange Announces Results for Q2 2022," press release, August 19, 2022e; Moscow Exchange, "Moscow Exchange Announces Results for Q3 2022," press release, November 3, 2022f.
NOTE: The Moscow Exchange press releases provide different dollar amounts than those listed in the table. Although the 2021 amounts likely reflect true value because the ruble was freely traded, we do not believe the 2022 values do so, as explained in the text. Accordingly, we converted all ruble amounts at the rate of 76 to the dollar. The amounts given by the Moscow Exchange are as follows (all in billions of U.S. dollars): Q4 2020, $695; Q1 2021, $746; Q2 2021, $818; Q3 2021, $894; Q4 2021, $842; Q1 2022, $579; Q2 2022, $779; and Q3 2022, $588. Q = quarter, and 1, 2, 3, and 4 stand for the specific quarter.

We did not have an equivalent measure of the total valuation of Russian bonds. However, the Moscow Stock Exchange provides data on the capitalization of the aggregate bond index, symbol RUABITR. Here again, there was significant value destruction, but, unlike with equities, the total capitalization of the bond index rebounded by mid-year and still ended up at a higher value

---

[34] Note that the Moscow Exchange press release records dollar value changes for the first quarter of 2022 as a decline of $263 billion and for the second quarter of 2022 as an *increase* of $200 billion.

at the end of September than at the beginning of 2022, despite a decline in the third quarter of 2022 (Table 2.4).[35]

Table 2.4. Capitalization of the Moscow Exchange Aggregate Bond Index (RUABITR)

Date	Value in Trillions of Rubles	Value in Billions of Dollars
December 29, 2021	11.43	150
March 31, 2022	9.99	131
June 30, 2022	11.59	153
September 29, 2022	10.46	137

SOURCE: Moscow Exchange, "RUABITR Bond Index," webpage, 2022h.
NOTE: As is done elsewhere in this paper, ruble values are converted to dollars at the rate of 76 rubles per dollar.

Human Capital Destruction

Russia's invasion of Ukraine accelerated exits from Russia, but exact numbers are uncertain. In addition, service in the war removed people from the labor market. Consequences for the Russian economy are negative.

As of the beginning of August 2022, one estimate held that about 150,000 to 300,000 people had left Russia since the war started.[36] Those exiting the country because of the war appear to be younger and better educated or higher skilled than the general Russian population.[37] One survey in March 2022 found that about half worked in information technology with an additional 16 percent each in management and the arts and culture.[38] In addition, one Russian trade association reported in May 2022 that about 10 percent of Russia's technology workforce had left or was planning to leave.[39]

Official statistics for January through March 2022 found departures abroad much higher than for the same period in 2021, including to Georgia (38,281 versus 8,504), Estonia (125,426 versus 29,364), Latvia (25,568 versus 13,521), and Armenia (134,129 versus 44,586).[40] Emigration was also much larger to Central Asian countries that traditionally send migrant labor, including

---

[35] The loss of valuation of bonds is not the only debt security-related event caused by the war. In June 2022, Russia defaulted on external bonds for the first time since 1918 (Giulia Morpurgo and Libby Cherry, "Russia Slips into Historic Default as Sanctions Muddy Next Steps," Bloomberg, June 26, 2022). Notably, Russia had the money available to pay interest to creditors but could not do so because of sanctions. In addition, this was less a cost to the Russian economy than to the foreign creditors who were owed the interest payments.

[36] "Much of Russia's Intellectual Elite Has Fled the Country," *The Economist*, August 9, 2022.

[37] "Anti-War Wave [АНТИВОЕННАЯ ВОЛНА]," OK Russians, webpage, 2022.

[38] "Much of Russia's Intellectual Elite Has Fled the Country," 2022.

[39] Yvonne Lau, "'We Realized That There's No Way We Can Return': Russia's Best and Brightest are Leaving the Country in Record Numbers. 6 Young Russians Explain Why They Left," *Fortune*, August 20, 2022.

[40] "Nearly 4M Russians Left Russia in Early 2022—FSB," *Moscow Times*, May 6, 2022.

Tajikistan (40,054 versus 8,857) and Uzbekistan (53,084 versus 15,026). These latter workers are unlikely to fit the profile of the people who have left for Europe.

Even using the high estimate of people who have left Russia—300,000—it is not clear that this will have serious economic costs, for two reasons. First, the prime working-age population, ages 25 to 54, was estimated to be 60.6 million in 2022.[41] Accordingly, those who left amount to slightly less than half of 1 percent, and not all leavers were in this age group, so the proportion was likely lower. This could increase but would still be a small proportion of the prime working-age population and an even smaller proportion of the total working-age population, ages 15 to 64, which was estimated at 94.2 million in 2022.

Second, even if many of these leavers were high-skilled, it is not clear that their skills would be useful in a sanctions-constrained economy.

> Of course, highly educated labor force is a plus. But that labor, in order to produce its maximum, needs also to work with top technology. If top technology is unavailable . . . , highly educated labor will be wasted. Due to the shrinking population, even the overall pool of such labor will every years [sic] be smaller. Since it will not find adequate use and adequate pay in Russia it will tend to emigrate thus further shrinking the available number of highly skilled workers.[42]

This suggests that the costs to Russia of the emigration, at least in the near term, will be low, though not negligible. However, in the longer term, emigration, especially if it increases substantially, is one more element that will slowly grind down the Russian economy to underperformance relative not only to its prewar potential but also to the technologically advanced countries of the world.[43]

Service in the war itself will also lead to human capital destruction in three ways. First, those killed in action (KIA) will represent a net loss to the labor force. Second, those wounded might be less productive if they do not recover fully. We provide details in Chapter 3 on numbers killed and wounded. Finally, those serving might be losing skills relevant to the civilian economy, or not gaining skills they would have otherwise gained through on-the-job-training or education. Even though they might gain training or education after service, even the time delay is a human capital cost to the economy. Together, emigration and war-related human capital destruction are

---

[41] United States Census Bureau, 2021.

[42] Branko Milanovic, "Russia's Long-Term Economic Prospects," *Global Inequality and More 3.0*, March 11, 2022a.

[43] Interestingly, Russia appears to be trying to encourage migration into Russia, at least according to a video posted by the Embassy of Russia to Spain on July 29, 2022. The video runs for 53 seconds and shows various pictures of Russia with the narrator saying, "This is Russia. Delicious cuisine. Beautiful women. Cheap gas. Rich history. World-famous literature. Unique architecture. Fertile soil. Cheap electricity and water. Ballet. Cheap taxi and delivery. Traditional values. Christianity. No cancel culture. Hospitality. Vodka. Economy that can withstand thousands of sanctions. Time to move to Russia! Don't delay . . . Winter is coming." However, rather than encouraging people to move to Russia, the video is just as likely trolling the United States ("no cancel culture") and threatening Europe with a potential gas cutoff ("Winter is coming") (Rusia en España [@EmbajadaRusaES], "Time to move to Russia," Twitter post, July 29, 2022).

likely to be negative for the Russian economy, but the magnitude of their drag on economic performance is uncertain.

Looking Ahead

The sanctions and the war have proven costly to Russia through summer 2022. These costs will continue to mount, with both the Bank of Russia and the Ministry of Economic Development expecting decreases in annual GDP in 2022 and 2023. The Bank of Russia projected a decline of between 4 percent and 6 percent in 2022 and between 1 percent and 4 percent in 2023. The Ministry projected a decline of 4.2 percent in 2022 and 2.7 percent in 2023.[44] Both projected increases in 2024 and 2025.

Much of this—especially the more-positive projections in later years—will depend on the pace of the war and defense expenditures; Russia's ability to transform its economy to account for declines in imports; and, importantly, Russia's ability to continue selling oil and gas. In its July forecast, the Bank of Russia projected that annual import values through 2024 would be lower than in 2021, though they would be rising. It also projected export values would decline in both 2023 and 2024. Later in 2022, in its annual World Energy Outlook, the International Energy Agency projected that the net volume of Russian oil exports would decline from 7.2 million barrels per day in 2021 to slightly more than 6 million barrels per day in 2024 and 5.3 million barrels per day in 2030. Likewise, it projected that gas exports would fall from about 250 billion cubic meters in 2021 to about 155 billion cubic meters in 2024 and 140 billion cubic meters in 2030.[45] The actual pace is likely to be determined in large part by actions of the Western countries determined to support Ukraine in its war effort.

---

[44] Bank of Russia, 2022n; "Russian Economy Ministry Expects Inflation to Reach 13.4% in 2022, GDP to Drop to 4.2%," TASS, August 16, 2022.

[45] International Energy Agency, World Energy Outlook 2022, Paris, "Russian Oil Exports in the World Energy Outlook, 2022 vs. 2021," webpage, last updated October 26, 2022; International Energy Agency, World Energy Outlook 2022, Paris, "Russian Gas Exports in the World Energy Outlook, 2022 vs. 2021," webpage, last updated November 3, 2022.

Chapter 3. Direct Military Costs

Calculating the direct cost of a military campaign can be straightforward. The United States in April 2003 passed a supplemental spending bill for the Iraq war totaling $54.4 billion through September 2003. This was in support of combat operations led by 149,000 U.S. ground troops as of August 2003.[46] A publicly available House of Commons estimate put the cost of the British air campaign in Libya at $512 million (320 million pounds), including costs for replacing expended munitions.[47]

Russia's war in Ukraine began with a similar number of ground forces as the Iraq war, and it has sustained air operations at varying degrees of intensity throughout the conflict. There is very little public information from Russia, however, about increased outlays in support of military operations. As the war has gone on, Russia has restricted information about the war. Most often it is the indirect costs of the war that are cause for debate; in Russia's war, we know very little officially about the direct costs.

A useful data point came from a Russian Ministry of Finance report on defense spending from January 2022 through April 2022.[48] In March 2022, Russia spent 450 billion rubles ($5.9 billion) on "national defense."[49] In March 2021 and March 2020, Russia spent an average of 364 billion rubles, for an increase of 86 billion rubles in 2022. In April 2022, Russia spent 627 billion rubles on national defense, compared with an average of 233 billion rubles over the same month in 2021 and 2020, for an increase of 394 billion rubles.[50] Using these data, we constructed a rough estimate that Russia in the first months of the war spent perhaps 240 billion rubles ($3.1 billion) per month for operations in Ukraine.[51] Over the course of seven months, that works out to approximately 1.68 trillion rubles, or $22.1 billion. Rough estimates of topline figures only tell us so much about Russian costs to date, however. Exploring Russian direct military costs

---

[46] Amy Belasco, *The Cost of Iraq, Afghanistan, and Other Global War on Terror Operations Since 9/11*, Congressional Research Service, RL33110, December 8, 2014.

[47] Gavin Berman, "The Cost of International Military Operations," Standard Note SN/SG/3139, United Kingdom House of Commons, July 5, 2012.

[48] Ivan Tkachev and Iuliia Vyrodova, "The Ministry of Finance in Connection with the Sanctions Classified Budget Expenditures in Areas [Минфин в связи с санкциями засекретил расходы бюджета по направлениям]," RBC, June 14, 2022.

[49] "Concise Information on the Execution of the Federal Budget [Краткая информация об исполнении федерального бюджета]," Russian Ministry of Finance, Spring 2022.

[50] Tkachev and Vyrodova, 2022.

[51] The March and April 2022 increases over Russia's average defense spending over the same time frame in 2021 and 2020 were 86 billion rubles and 394 billion rubles, respectively. The average of those two numbers is 240 billion rubles.

beyond the total number can offer a broader picture of what Putin's decision to invade Ukraine has meant for the Russian military and the federal budget.

There are several caveats to the figures presented in this chapter. In this chapter, we presented a rough order-of-magnitude estimate of the direct costs of the Russian military campaign in Ukraine. We relied on open-source information to generate our estimates; this being the case, we do not claim that our numbers are final or authoritative. Rather, our purpose is to offer a sense of what the direct military costs to Russia might be and inform a preliminary judgment on Russia's ability to sustain the war going forward.

Approach

Our approach to estimating direct costs of Russian military operations involved two elements. Because the war has been fought primarily on the ground and in the air, we focused on the cost for Russia to sustain ground and air operations. Next, we drew on available information to present weapons, equipment, and personnel losses and the replacement costs; we also considered the cost of high-end munitions such as air- and sea-launched cruise missiles and short-range ballistic missiles. This is roughly the same method the British used to calculate the costs of their participation in the 2011 Libya campaign. Our estimate of costs will not be comprehensive because our access to data was quite limited. But our findings can serve as a reference point to understand the effect of the direct costs on Russian finances and military, as well as on Russia's ability to continue the war.

Because we had some official data on overall costs of the war to Russia in March and April 2022 and because we had reasonable estimates of the cost of Russian air operations based on the recent precedent of the Syria intervention, we used some simple math to estimate the cost of sustaining Russian ground operations (which were most difficult to determine with precision because of the lack of recent precedent and information) and the overall cost including weapon replacement costs and additional payments made to soldiers, families, and mobilized troops. This approach was neither comprehensive nor definitive, but it provided a deeper look at the direct costs of the war to Russia using available data. Our findings are summarized in Table 3.1.

Table 3.1. Cost to Russia of Military Operations

Cost Category	Cost Breakdown
Operations	Seven months of air operations and ground operations $\approx$ 1.68 trillion rubles
Materiel	Precision munitions replacement cost and combat weapons and equipment/loss replacement cost $\approx$ 0.8 trillion rubles
Compensation	Combat, reserve, mercenary, and compensatory pay $\approx$ 0.5 trillion rubles
Total	$\approx$ 3.01 trillion rubles

Cost of Russian Air Operations in Ukraine

According to an estimate by RBC, a Russian business news outlet, in late 2015, Russia was spending approximately 4.6 billion rubles per month to conduct primarily air operations in Syria.[52] Russia in that campaign was conducting 40 sorties per day, on average, and supporting mostly noncombat duties of 1,600 personnel. In the Ukraine war, Russia's combat sortie rate has been roughly 250 per day, or six times that of Syria.[53] Using the Syria campaign as a rough guide, we estimated a per-month cost of 27.6 billion rubles for Russia to conduct 250 daily combat sorties.[54] Extended to the first seven months of the war, Russia's air operations might have cost roughly 193.2 billion rubles (or $2.5 billion at a 76-to-1 ruble-dollar exchange rate) over that period, with allowances that Russia's sortie rate varied over time.

Air and Rotary Losses

A major difference between Ukraine and Syria is the amount of combat losses Russia has suffered. The Oryx website tracked 56 Russian aircraft, 49 helicopters, and 127 unmanned aerial vehicles (UAVs) destroyed or captured as of September 19, 2022. With some exclusions, the losses by aircraft type are shown in Table 3.2.

---

[52] Maksim Solopov and Aleksandr Artem'ev, "RBC Investigation: How Much Is Russia Spending on its War in Syria? [Расследование РБК: сколько тратит Россия на войну в Сирии]," RBC, October 28, 2015. For reference, IHS Jane's calculated that Russia was spending $120 million per month to maintain and operate 36 combat aircraft and 20 helicopters. Janes, in its estimate, stated that Russia was flying an average of 40 sorties per day. See Peter Hobson, "Calculating the Cost of Russia's War in Syria," *Moscow Times*, October 20, 2015.

[53] Tara Copp, "Russian Jets Flying 200 Sorties a Day, but Firing from Their Own Airspace, Pentagon Says," *Defense One*, March 11, 2022; James Beardsworth, "Uptick in Combat Missions Signals Changing Role for Russia's Air Force in Ukraine," *Moscow Times*, May 11, 2022.

[54] 4.6 billion rubles x 6 = 27.6 billion rubles per month in Ukraine.

Table 3.2. Russian Fixed- and Rotary-Wing Losses in Ukraine War as of Mid-September 2022

Aircraft Name	Aircraft Type	Losses	Cost Per Aircraft (Millions of Rubles)	Total Cost (Millions of Rubles)	Cost Per Aircraft (Millions of Dollars)	Total Cost (Millions of Dollars)
Su-25	Combat	22	400	8,800	5.2	115.8
Su-24MR	Reconnaissance	1	418	418	5.5	5.5
Su-24M	Bomber	6	418	2,508	5.5	33.0
Su-30SM	Combat	11	1,180	5,900	15.5	77.6
Su-35S	Combat	1	2,280	2,280	30.0	30.0
Su-34/M	Combat	13	1,200	10,200	15.7	134.2
An-26	Transport	1	11	11	0.144	0.1
Mi-8	Rotary transport	12	252	3,000	3.3	39.5
Mi-24P	Rotary attack	3	Unk	Unk	Unk	Unk
Mi-35M	Rotary attack	5	566	2,264	7.4	29.8
Mi-28	Rotary attack	6	1,162	5,810	15.2	76.4
Ka-52	Rotary attack	17	857	12,855	11.2	169.1
Unknown	Rotary	6	861[a]	5,166	11.3	68.0
Orlan-10	Reconnaissance/EW UAV	84	18	1,512	0.236	19.9
Total		188	n/a	60,724	n/a	799.0

SOURCE: Stijn Mitzer and Jakub Janovsky, in collaboration with Joost Oliemans, Kemall, Dan, and naalsio26, "Attack on Europe: Documenting Russian Equipment Losses During the 2022 Russian Invasion of Ukraine," Oryx, August 2, 2022. Information on the Su-25 is from "New Su-25: The Cost of the 'Supergracha' Has Been Revealed [Новый Су-25: стала известна стоимость «Суперграча»]," Warfiles.ru, August 31, 2022. Information on the Su-30SM and Su-35S is from Anton Lavrov and Bogdan Stepovoi, "'Superalligator' for a Billion Rubles: The Ministry of Defense Confirmed the Price of New Helicopters [«Суперааллигатор» за миллиард: Минобороны утвердило цену новых вертолетов], *Izvestiya*, October 4, 2021. Information on the Su-34 is from: Sebastien Roblin, "Russia Is Upgrading Its Supersonic Su-34 'Hellduck' Bombers," *National Interest*, May 15, 2021. Information on the An-26 is from "The Belorussian Military Is Selling Two An-26 Aircraft [Белорусские военные продают два самолета Ан-26]," *RIA Novosti*, February 13, 2014. Information on the Mi-34M is from "The FSB is Buying Five Mi-35M Helicopters [ФСБ России закупит пять вертолетов Ми-35М]," Centre for Analysis of Strategy and Technologies, blog post, July 9, 2015. Information on the Mi-28 is from Inna Siderkova, "The Ministry of Defense Will Receive 24 'Flying Tanks' to Test in Syria [Минобороны получит 24 «летающих танка» для испытания в Сирии]," RBC, October 19, 2017. Note that this is the price for a modernized Mi-28NM; in Mitzer and Janovsky (2022), the helicopter is described only as Mi-28. Information on the Ka-52 is from "The Ministry of Defense Will Buy 140 Ka-52 Helicopters [Минобороны купит более 140 вертолётов Ка-52]," RBC, September 3, 2011. Information on the Orlan-10 is from Vladimir Tuchkov, "Whose UAVs Are the Best: Israeli, American, or Russian? [Чьи беспилотники лучше: израильские, американские или российские?]," *Svobodnaya Pressa*, November 2, 2014.

NOTE: Exchange rate: 76 rubles to 1 US dollar. Prices are not official, might not correspond to the exact variant lost in Ukraine, and should be considered approximate. Unk = unknown; EW = electronic warfare.

[a] 861 million rubles is the average cost of the three previous helicopters listed in the table.

Overall Cost Estimate of Air Operations and Combat Losses

To recap, we estimated that the cost of sustaining Russian air operations—250 sorties per day— over the first seven months of the war was approximately 193.2 billion rubles, or $2.5 billion. When we added the cost of aircraft, rotary, and Orlan UAV losses, the cost rose to approximately 253.9 billion rubles, or $3.3 billion. As a rough point of comparison, the United

States spent just over a billion dollars in the Libya campaign in which it flew over 7,000 sorties (1,600 of which were strike sorties) and did not suffer any casualties.[55]

Ground Operations

Russia's invasion of Ukraine brought together the largest contingent of ground forces in Europe since World War II. At the same time, how many Russian troops crossed the border into Ukraine is still a matter of discussion.[56] Initial U.S. estimates put the Russian ground force at 150,000 to 190,000 troops, but more-recent analysis based on Russian personnel rosters leaked by the Ukrainians suggested that the number might have been closer to 120,000.[57] The Ukrainian defense minister similarly announced on February 18, 2022, that Russia's land forces around Ukraine numbered 129,000.[58] A Russian paratrooper who reportedly participated in the Kherson attack in the south of Ukraine from Crimea estimated total Russian ground troops could have been as few as 100,000.[59] The discrepancy results largely from the uncertainty of the actual number of Russian troops in combat formations versus the initial estimates based on Russian self-reporting. Russian battalion tactical groups (BTGs), for example, might in some cases have fielded as few as 400 troops.[60] Russia analysts prior to the war often assumed 750 personnel per BTG, on average, using comments by the chief of the Russian General Staff, Valerii Gerasimov.[61]

Thus, it is possible that the Russians invaded with a force that was understrength from what the Russian military had advertised in the years leading up to the war. To be conservative on cost, we worked from the lower bound of 120,000 official Russian land troops to conduct operations in Ukraine. Reports on the number of Donbas separatist forces range from 20,000 to 40,000.[62] While there is little concrete evidence that Russia is paying these fighters from Luhansk and Donetsk, according to a 2016 interview with Alexander Khodakovsky, a former

---

[55] Karl Mueller, ed., *Precision and Purpose: Air Power in the Libyan Civil War*, RAND Corporation, RR-676-AF, 2011, pp. 146; 380.

[56] Michael Kofman and Rob Lee, "Not Built for Purpose: The Russian Military's Ill-Fated Force Design," *War on the Rocks*, June 2, 2022.

[57] Kofman and Lee, 2022.

[58] "The Troops of the Russian Federation Near Ukraine Number About 149,000 People and May Increase by Several Thousand More in the Coming Days [Війська РФ поблизу України налічують близько 149 тис. осіб і найближчими днями можуть зрости ще на кілька тисяч]," Interfax-Ukraine, February 18, 2022.

[59] Pavel Filatiev, *ZOV*, Vkontakte, August 1, 2022.

[60] V. V. Grachev, "Analysis of the Problems of Material Support of the Battalion Tactical Group Revealed During a Special Exercise with Military Governance Bodies, Brigades, Military Units and Logistics Organizations of the Central Military District," *Herald of the Volsk Military Institute of Logistics*, Vol. 2, No. 38, 2016.

[61] "Contractees in BTGs," *Russian Defense Policy*, blog post, September 17, 2016.

[62] David Axe, "In 100 Days, a Separatist Army in Ukraine Lost Half Its Troops," *Forbes*, June 13, 2022a; Interfax-Ukraine, "Kyiv Says There Are About 6,000 Russian Soldiers, 40,000 Separatists in Donbas," *Kyiv Post*, September 11, 2017.

separatist minister, "Without outside help, it's impossible to sustain the territory even if you have the most effective tax-raising system. The level of help from Russia exceeds the amounts that we collect within the territory."[63] This suggests that Moscow could not count on the loyalty of these fighters without directly financing them. Further, as Russia took losses of regular forces as the war progressed, reports appeared detailing Russian attempts to recruit mercenaries.[64]

The two sections that follow explore the cost of sustaining that number of ground troops and the losses in weapons and equipment up to August 2, 2022.

Cost of Sustainment of Ground Operations

Estimating the cost of Russian ground operations is a challenge. First, the war has changed in content and scope. In February, Russia invaded along four axes throughout southern and eastern Ukraine. In early April, Russian land forces withdrew from the Kyiv area and concentrated in the east and south, where the war became largely an artillery duel (supported by air strikes) with slow-going Russian advances. In addition, the Russian force grouping took a vastly different shape. As of late July 2022, a U.S. estimate of Russian casualties (killed and wounded) was 75,000, an estimate that likely included both Russian and Russian-affiliated land forces.[65] Finally, there were no data about the day-to-day operating costs of Russian ground and airborne forces in peacetime. Such information could serve as a baseline reference point.

Cross-country comparisons are also problematic. As noted above, the ground portion of the U.S. invasion of Iraq with a similar sized force contingent cost roughly $10 billion per month for the initial phase of the campaign. But the United States spends more on combat operations than Russia given the differences in cost of goods, services, bonuses, and contractor pay, among others.[66]

Combat pay is only one cost driver of sustaining ground-based combat operations. Ammunition and fuel are other expensive inputs. At the same time, we did not have much data related to either the amount or the cost of these critical supplies that Russia is consuming in its ground operations. Nevertheless, we address portions of these cost categories below, which could serve as a starting point for future analysis.

---

[63] Anton Zverev, "Moscow is Bankrolling Ukraine Rebels: Ex-Separatist Official," Reuters, October 5, 2016.

[64] Julian Borger, "Russia Deploys Up to 20,000 Mercenaries in Battle for Ukraine's Donbas Region," *The Guardian*, April 19, 2022.

[65] Michael Schwirtz, Marc Santora, and Matthew Mpoke Bigg, "Ukraine Pushes to Retake Ground in the South as Russia Pours in Reinforcements," *New York Times*, July 28, 2022.

[66] Heidi Peltier, *The Growth of the 'Camo Economy' and the Commercialization of the Post-9/11 Wars*, Watson Institute at Brown University and Pardee Center at Boston University, June 30, 2020.

Pay

Regular Forces Combat Pay

Regular military pay and combat pay is highly variable. Rank, specialization, and other factors mean that even similar service members are receiving different paychecks. But an average Russian sergeant with five years' experience might receive around 50,000 rubles per month, or $657.[67] According to a Russian paratrooper, just prior to the invasion, a commander informed a unit in Crimea that regular soldier pay would be increased to around 200,000 rubles per month, or $2,723—a 400-percent increase if using the average sergeant's base pay.[68] If Russia were to pay an average of 150,000 additional rubles per month to 100,000 soldiers, that would amount to 15 billion rubles, or $197 million per month. Over seven months, the total in combat pay would be 105 billion rubles ($1.4 billion). To be sure, there are reports that Russia is not paying soldiers what it committed to.[69]

Reserve Pay and Bonuses

As noted above, Russia likely sustained steep losses in personnel during its first seven months of war in Ukraine. Since perhaps April or May 2022, Russia has been engaged in efforts to stand up new units to send to Ukraine to relieve soldiers on the front line and to replace lost formations. According to *Kommersant*, a Russian business daily, Russia as of early August was in the midst of a multi-month effort to form at least 40 volunteer battalions.[70] Russia was forming these battalions on a territorial basis, with most oblasts (provinces) recruiting and training at least one formation. To recruit volunteers, Russia was offering inflated monthly salaries and bonuses, which vary by area. The salaries are 170,000 rubles per month ($2,236). Bonuses range from 200,000 to 300,000 rubles.[71] If each battalion has 500 troops—a typical maneuver battalion strength, on paper—pay for these personnel over seven months would total 23.8 billion rubles ($313.1 million). One-time bonuses, at an average of 250,000 rubles, add an additional 5 billion rubles ($65.7 million).

Likely in response to Russian defeats on the battlefield, on September 21, 2022, President Vladmir Putin announced a partial mobilization of 300,000 reservists.[72] At this early juncture, it

---

[67] "Contract Service [Служба по контракту]," Soyuz Prizyvnikov Rossii, August 31, 2022.

[68] Filatiev, 2022.

[69] Gerrard Kaonga, "Russia Failing to Properly Pay, Feed Military Recruits in Ukraine—Report," *Newsweek*, August 15, 2022.

[70] Andrei Vinokurov, "Special Volunteer Operation [Специальная добровольческая операция]," *Kommersant*, August 8, 2022.

[71] Stanislav Shemelov and Maksim Kirilov, "The Word 'Battalion' Is Too Much: How the Named Units Are Standing in for Mobilization in Russia [Слово «батальон» здесь чересчур преувеличено»: как именные подразделения заменяют в России мобилизацию]," *BiznesOnline*, August 24, 2022.

[72] "Mobilization and the SMO (Special Military Operation). The Key Points of Sergei Shoigu's Speech [Мобилизация и СВО. Главные тезисы выступления Сергея Шойгу]," Smotrim.ru, September 21, 2022.

is not clear how Russia plans to integrate mobilized troops into the fight. Will they be formed into wholly new units? Will they be equipped with weapons and equipment from storage bases? Will the military-industrial complex need to supply them with new kit? Will these new troops mostly strengthen existing units and serve as infantry forces? In all likelihood, there will be some combination of these options. But it is difficult to estimate a cost for all the mobilization tasks required to get 300,000 troops to the battlefield.

What we know with more certainty is that mobilized forces will be treated as those serving under contract.[73] Thus, we used 170,000 rubles as our average pay for Russia's mobilization forces. At the same time, it is unlikely that Russia will manage to call up 300,000 troops all at once, if they manage to achieve that number at all. Presumably, mobilization will be a phased process that could take a year or more.[74] Thus, not every mobilized reserve will begin being paid in September 2022. For the 300,000 troops that were mobilized following the September announcement, the monthly cost in salaries will be roughly 51 billion rubles ($671 million).

Mercenary Pay

In March 2022, Putin approved moving 16,000 fighters from the Middle East to support Russia's war in Ukraine. The average pay for soldiers was $200 to $300 per month to work as security guards, according to the Associated Press.[75] If a recruit had combat experience, the total sum increased to $3,000. It does not appear that any large influx of Middle East recruits ever materialized, however.[76] There is better evidence on the participation of Wagner mercenaries on the Russian side. There were reportedly around 1,000 such fighters in Ukraine as of mid-August 2022.[77] According to Yevgeniy Nuzhnin, a former prison inmate who joined Wagner and then immediately surrendered after deploying, the salary for fighting in Ukraine was 100,000 rubles per month.[78] To pay 1,000 fighters for seven months at that salary would total 700 million rubles ($9.2 million).

In all, estimated compensation outlays including combat pay for active forces (300,000 mobilized), inflated pay and bonuses for reserves, and Wagner mercenary pay come to 185.5 billion rubles ($2.4 billion).

---

[73] President of Russia, Decree on the Announcement of Partial Mobilization in the Russian Federation [Указ «Об объявлении частичной мобилизации в Российской Федерации»]," Decree No. 647, September 21, 2022.

[74] V. M. Maskin, "On the Issue of Maintaining Constant Readiness Formations and Combat Units [К вопросу о содержании соединенийеи воинских частей в категории постоянной готовности]," *Military Thought*, No. 1, 2010.

[75] Zeina Karam, "Explainer: Will Russia Bring Syrian Fighters to Ukraine?" Associated Press, March 11, 2022.

[76] Pierre Boussel, "Syrian Mercenaries in Ukraine: Delusion or Reality," *Sada*, Carnegie Endowment for International Peace, June 23, 2022.

[77] "What Is Russia's Wagner Group of Mercenaries in Ukraine?" BBC, August 16, 2022.

[78] "'If You Didn't Follow Instructions, They Shot You': A Russian Convict Recruited by the Wagner Group Tells His Story," *Meduza.io*, September 16, 2022.

By presidential decree, Russia is supposed to compensate the families of fallen soldiers as well as soldiers severely wounded in action. For those KIA, the families are entitled to a total compensation of 7.42 million rubles ($97,644).[79] Those who are severely wounded receive 3 million rubles ($39,473), although reporting has questioned whether all injured Russian troops are receiving their due.[80] According to the United States, Russia as of mid-August had suffered up to 80,000 casualties since the war began.[81] Using the traditional ratio of 3 wounded to 1 killed, that suggests Russia has suffered 20,000 KIA and 60,000 wounded, although the number has certainly climbed through late September 2022. To determine the total cost of the compensation program, however, we needed detailed information on how many of those killed and seriously wounded were active-duty Russian soldiers. Based on the 3 wounded to 1 killed ratio, the cost of compensation to all the families of those KIA would be 148.4 billion rubles, or around $2 billion. Payouts to wounded soldiers would be an additional 180 billion rubles ($2.3 billion), although some wounded soldiers probably would not qualify for this.

Pay Summary

In all, our total estimate for seven months of combat pay, reserve pay and bonuses, one month mobilization pay for 300,000 troops, mercenary pay, and compensation to families is 513.9 billion rubles, or $6.7 billion. To be sure, the number of seriously wounded Russian soldiers is unknown, and our estimate of the seriously wounded might have been high. At the same time, we did not calculate the follow-on costs for long-term care of seriously wounded soldiers.

Artillery

Since the beginning of the war, artillery has been the primary destructive instrument for both sides. One prewar analysis of the Russian military described it as an "artillery army with a lot of combat vehicles."[82] Nothing that has happened since late February 2022 has provided any reason to question that description. According to a report from the Royal United Services Institute in early July 2022, "Russia [was] firing approximately 20,000 152-mm artillery shells per day compared with Ukraine's 6,000, with an even greater proportional disparity in multiple rocket

[79] Maria Lisitsyna, "Putin Revealed Compensation Figures to Injured and Families of Fallen Soldiers in Ukraine [Путин раскрыл выплаты раненым и семьям погибших на Украине военных]," RBC, March 3, 2022.

[80] Maria Tsvetkova, "Some Wounded Russian Soldiers Find Compensation Elusive, Despite Putin's Pledge," Reuters, July 29, 2022.

[81] Helene Cooper, "Heavy Losses Leave Russia Short of Its Goal, U.S. Officials Say," *New York Times*, August 11, 2022.

[82] Lester W. Grau and Charles K. Bartles, *The Russian Way of War: Force Structure, Tactics, and Modernization of the Russian Ground Forces*, Foreign Military Studies Office, 2016, p. 143.

launchers (MRLs) and missiles fired."[83] The Ukrainian military claimed in late June 2022 that the total Russian artillery expenditure was 60,000 shells per day at that time.[84] Once through the initial Russian gambit to rapidly seize control of Kyiv and large population centers throughout much of Ukraine, the war devolved, roughly speaking, into an artillery duel to take small chunks of territory at a grinding pace.

Can Russia sustain an artillery war of this intensity? In short, the central issue is not cost because regular artillery shells are not very expensive relative to other military weaponry. Russia has over a million tons of shells it can draw on from storage, and it can produce more domestically and procure internationally to some extent.[85] The more relevant question is the survivability and sustainment of the artillery systems themselves, which likely cost a few million dollars per item in the case of newer systems, such as variants of the 2S19 152 mm howitzer.[86] *Forbes* reported in late July 2022 that Russia had lost over 300 artillery pieces in the war.[87] At the same time, Russia has thousands of pieces of rocket artillery and self-propelled howitzers in its inventory to throw into what has become a protracted war of attrition in Ukraine.[88]

Fuel

In late May 2022, commodities analysts who follow the Russian fuel market offered estimates of Russian fuel consumption in the war to that point. Typically, Russian monthly diesel output is about 6.7 million metric tons.[89] Beginning in December 2021, output increased by 9 percent compared with December 2020. January 2022 saw a similar change. Reportedly, Russia "stopped publishing any production data" after the start of the war, but Russian diesel demand throughout the first quarter of 2022 was considerably higher than 2021, with the war "consuming almost 6% of Russia's total diesel refining output."[90] With regard to total fuel consumption, one

---

[83] Jack Watling and Nick Reynolds, *Special Report: Ukraine at War: Paving the Road from Survival to Victory*, Royal United Services Institute for Defence and Security Studies, July 4, 2022.

[84] Isabelle Khurshudyan and Paul Sonne, "Russia Targeted Ukrainian Ammunition to Weaken Kyiv on the Battlefield," *Washington Post*, June 24, 2022.

[85] Hlib Parfonov, "Ukrainian Strikes Cause Moscow to Re-Think Munitions Supply and Logistics (Part Two)," *Eurasia Daily Monitor*, Vol. 19, No. 127, August 18, 2022; "In Russia, Ammunition Stocks Were Created for 70 Years: A Military Expert Told How Much They Would be Enough," *West Observer*, July 26, 2022.

[86] "MSTA-SV," Deagel.com, August 31, 2022.

[87] David Axe, "The Russian Army Has Lost More Than 300 Artillery Pieces in Ukraine. Old Howitzers Could Replace Them," *Forbes*, July 27, 2022b.

[88] Edward Geist, "Appendix F: Indirect Fires," in Andrew Radin, Lynn E. Davis, Edward Geist, Eugeniu Han, Dara Massicot, Matthew Povlock, Clint Reach, Scott Boston, Samuel Charap, William Mackenzie, Katya Migacheva, Trevor Johnston, and Austin Long, *The Future of the Russian Military: Russia's Ground Combat Capabilities and Implications for U.S.-Russia Competition*, RAND Corporation, RR-3099-A, 2018.

[89] Rosemary Griffin, Elza Turner, Nick Coleman, and Alexander Bor, "Ukraine War Sees Diesel Prices Rise as Russia's Thirsty Battle Tanks Guzzle Fuel," S&P Global Commodity Insights, May 23, 2022.

[90] Griffin et al., 2022.

analyst estimated that Russia as of late May 2022 had consumed roughly 15 million liters per day of all fuels for the war up to that point.[91] Simply using the price of a liter of Russian diesel fuel—approximately $0.90—for 180 days of war Russia might have spent $2.43 billion on fuel. This is a crude estimate, because the 15 million liter per day figure is only one analyst's view, and we did not have any information on the amounts of other types of fuel consumed.

Cost of Ground Weapons and Equipment Losses

Another cost to Russia comes in the form of weapons and equipment losses of the Ground Forces and Airborne. Many analysts use the Oryx website, which has been tracking Russian and Ukrainian losses since the beginning of the war. Oryx methodology "includes destroyed vehicles and equipment of which photo or videographic evidence is available. Small arms, ATGMs [anti-tank guided missiles], MANPADS [man-portable air defense systems], loitering munitions, drones used as unmanned bait, civilian vehicles, trailers and derelict equipment are not included . . ."[92]

We took the Oryx data and added cost in rubles and converted to dollars using a rate of 76 rubles to the dollar. None of our cost data are official. At best, we used Russian military press reporting on the details of contracts concluded between industry and the Ministry of Defense. Those reports sometimes provided enough information to determine a price per copy. More often, we relied on reports from Russian articles that did not always provide a source for the pricing data for weapons or equipment. In these, it was not clear if the authors were providing the cost to the Russian Ministry of Defense or the export cost, which could be considerably higher.

Our approach was to use replacement cost as the measure of cost to Russia. If Russia loses a T-72B main battle tank (MBT) manufactured in the 1990s, we assumed that loss will eventually be replaced by a modern tank. The same is true for armored fighting vehicles (AFVs), infantry fighting vehicles (IFVs), armored personnel carriers (APCs), self-propelled artillery (SPA), and MRLs.[93] Russian Ground and Airborne Forces are losing many other types of systems, but we limited our analysis to the above. The replacement systems we used are shown in Table 3.3, which reflects what we believed to be the most-likely systems for Russia to be fielding in the near term. Equipment losses and estimated costs are shown in Table 3.4.

---

[91] Griffin et al., 2022.

[92] Mitzer and Janovsky et al., 2022.

[93] It is possible that Russia might replace materiel at less than a one-to-one ratio given the increased expense and technology required. This would, of course, reduce Russia's replacement costs relative to our estimates.

Table 3.3. Selected Russian Ground Forces Systems and Replacements

System Category	Replacement System
MBT	T-90M
AFV	MT-LB
IFV	BMP-3
APC	BTR-82A
SPA	2S19M2
MRL	Tornado-G (122mm)

Table 3.4. Selected Russian Ground Losses in Ukraine War, as of September 19, 2022

Type	Losses	Unofficial Replacement Cost Per Item (Millions of Rubles)[a]	Total Replacement Cost (Billions of Rubles)	Cost Per Item (Millions of Dollars)	Total Replacement Cost (Millions of Dollars)
Main Battle Tank	1,155	300.0	346.50	3.900[b]	4,559.0
AFV	600	2.9[c]	1.74	0.038	22.8
IFV	1,280	85.0[d]	108.80	1.100	1,431.0
APC	162	28.0[e]	4.53	0.368	59.6
SPA	206	235.6[f]	48.40	3.100	636.8
MRL	109	32.0[g]	3.48	0.421	45.8
Total	3,512	n/a	513.40	n/a	6,755.2

SOURCE: Mitzer and Janovsky et al., 2022.
NOTE: 76 rubles to the U.S. dollar; Russian losses in these areas include both old and new equipment. To simplify, we used replacement cost, because Russia will be replacing losses with newer systems such as the T-90A MBT, the MT-LBVM APC, the BMP-3 IFV, and the BTR-82A(M). n/a = not applicable.
[a] Dmitrii Litovkin, "The T-72 Tanks Got the 'Relikt' [Танкам T-72 прописали «Реликт»]," *Izvestiya*, March 10, 2016.
[b] We did not know exactly what tank or tanks Russia will purchase to replace losses. However, the cost of a T-90M is reportedly around 300 million rubles, or $3.9 million at an exchange rate of 76 to 1. See "How Much Russian Military Armor Costs [Сколько стоит бронетехника Российской армии]," Ferra.ru, March 4, 2022. Another source stated that a T-90M cost roughly half that of a M1A2 SEP variant Abrams tank. According to the FY 2020 budget justification, the cost of an Abrams tank, based on the Forces Cost Model, was $5 million. See Sergei Suvorov, "The Ural 'Proryv': Why the New Russian T-90M is Worth Two Abrams [Уральский «Прорыв»: Почему новый российский танк т-90M стоит двух «Абрамсов»]," TVzvezda, February 2, 2018; Department of the Army, *Department of Defense Fiscal Year (FY) 2020 Budget Estimates, Procurement of Weapons and Tracked Combat Vehicles, Army*, March 2019.
[c] "MT-LB, Artillery Hauler. Its Cost [МТ-ЛБ" артиллерийский тягач. Его стоимость]," Zen.yandex, blog post, October 30, 2018.
[d] Based on the reported price of a BMP-3. See "How Much Russian Military Armor Costs [Сколько стоит бронетехника Российской армии]," 2022.
[e] "The Cost of the BTR-82A and Its Capabilities [Стоимость БТР-82А и его возможности]," Zen.yandex, blog post, October 11, 2018.
[f] "MSTA-SV," 2022.
[g] "Tornado-G MRL to Complete State Trials," *Janes*, undated.

Cost of Ground Operations Conclusion

Estimating the cost of ground operations is the least straightforward of the direct military cost areas we examined. There were many unknowns, no recent Russian precedent, and little sense of how much Russia spends to maintain its land forces in peacetime. The above at least gave a sense of the land-based losses to weapons and personnel Russia has sustained, and those have been staggering by modern standards. Russia's Ground Forces—approximately 275,000 at the start of the war—were historically small to begin with. The 15,000 to 25,000 KIA are not trivial numbers from an analytical perspective. Replacement of manpower, weapons, and equipment will take a minimum of a few years.

While our analysis did not support even a rough estimate, we used other evidence in this chapter to provide a sense of ground-based military costs for Russia. In the opening and closing sections of this chapter, we note that Russia in the early months of the war was probably spending around 240 billion rubles ($3.15 billion) per month in support of combat operations. In the section above, we estimated the cost of air operations to Russia at approximately 27.6 billion rubles ($363 million) per month. That would suggest, roughly speaking, 212 billion rubles, or $2.8 billion per month for ground operations, at least in the early months of the war. How that number has fluctuated over time as the war has changed in scope and scale is difficult to determine. We could hypothesize that the cost to Russia has decreased because of the smaller force size, smaller scale, and relatively static character of the conflict.

Cost of Long-Range Precision Weapons Expenditure

The final component of our analysis of the direct costs of military operations involved Russia's use of expensive long-range precision weapons. As in the other categories we examined above, some data exist, but they are incomplete. In the case of Russian use of conventional long-range weapons—air-, land-, and sea-based—there are estimates of total missiles expended and their types, but we did not know how many of each type of missile. As of July 21, 2022, Russia reportedly had used 3,219 missiles to attack targets across Ukraine.[94] But Russia has employed both the modern Iskander missile as well as its antecedent, the Tochka-U. If the former accounted for a large majority of Russian short-range ballistic missile launches, the expense would be considerably greater than if the ratio were reversed. According to a Ukrainian general officer in late June 2022, more than 50 percent of Russian missiles were from the Soviet era.[95] If one estimate from 2019 of around 1,500 modern Russian standoff weapons is proximate, then the proportion of Soviet weapons might well have increased in August because Russia theoretically would have exhausted its supply of modern long-range precision-guided munitions.[96] Moreover, analysts generally assume that Russia would keep some percentage of its modern long-range precision weapons in reserve for nuclear use.[97]

We used the above data from late July 2022 and the modern-legacy ratio as a means to approximate the cost to Russia as of that time—that is, 3,219 missiles, 1,600 of which we assumed were Soviet legacy weapons.[98] Tables 3.5 and 3.6 show the types and numbers of

[94] Center for Strategic and International Studies Missile Defense Project [@Missile_Defense], "Russian Missile Attacks on Ukraine," Twitter account, June 29, 2022.

[95] "Russia Ramping Up Ukraine Strikes with Less Precise Soviet-Era Missiles—General," Reuters, June 30, 2022.

[96] Fredrik Westerlund, Susanne Oxenstierna, Gudrun Persson, Jonas Kjellén, Johan Norberg, Jakob Hedenskog, Tomas Malmlöf, Martin Goliath, Johan Engvall, and Nils Dahlqvist, *Russian Military Capability in a Ten-Year Perspective 2019*, FOI, FOI-R-4758, 2019.

[97] Westerlund et al., 2019.

[98] A Reuters report, citing Ukrainian information, stated that Russia had fired 3,219 missiles as of July 21, 2022. However, it was not clear from the article how "cruise missiles" were distinguished from "air-to-surface missiles," which are not mutually exclusive. David Gauthier-Villars, Steve Stecklow, Maurice Tamman, Stephen Grey, and Andrew Macaskill, "As Russian Missiles Struck Ukraine, Western Tech Still Flowed," Reuters, August 8, 2022.

Russian missiles employed in Ukraine, with the numbers provided by Ukraine's National Security and Defense Council to Reuters. The Reuters data are categorized as cruise missiles, air-to-surface missiles, Iskander, Tochka-U, anti-radiation missiles, and P-800 Oniks. One challenge was that it is not clear how to distinguish between cruise missiles and air-to-surface missiles, which could be one and the same. The Kh-101 is an air-to-surface cruise missile, for example. Thus, there is the risk of double counting. As a workaround, we estimated a cost for a range from 1,816 to 3,219 missiles. The lower bound subtracts the 1,403 air-to-surface missiles.

Table 3.5. Russian Missiles Employed in Ukraine

Name (NATO)	Type	IOC	Range (km)	Employment in War
3M14 Kalibr (SS-N-30A)	SLCM	1994	1,000–1,500	Land attack
P-800 Oniks (SS-N-26)	ASCM	2002	320	Land attack
9M723 Iskander (SS-26)	SRBM	2006	500	Land attack
Tochka-U (SS-21)	SRBM	1989	120	Land attack
Kh-101 (n/a)	ALCM	2012	2,700	Land attack
Kh-55	ALCM	1983	2,400	Land attack
Kh-22	Anti-ship	1968	600	Land attack
Kh-31P	Anti-radiation	1988	110	Land attack
Kh-47M2	ALBM	2022	1,900	Land attack

SOURCES: Benjamin Brimelow, "Russia is Using Its Newest and Oldest Missiles Indiscriminately Against Ukraine," *Business Insider*, July 31, 2022;Gauthier-Villars et al., 2022; Rob Lee [@RALee85], "This looks like a Kh-31P air-launched anti-radar missile wreckage reportedly in Kyiv," Twitter post, February 23, 2022.
NOTE: IOC = initial operating capability; SLCM = sea-launched cruise missile; ASCM = anti-ship cruise missile; SRBM = short-range ballistic missile; ALCM = air-launched cruise missile; ALBM = air-launched ballistic missile.

Table 3.6. Reported Number of Russian Missiles Employed in Ukraine through August 2022

Missile Type	Number Employed
Cruise missile	1,486
Air-to-surface missile	1,403
Iskander	124
Tochka-U	66
Anti-radiation	35
P-800 Oniks	105
Total	3,219

SOURCE: Gauthier-Villars et al., 2022.

As with Russian ground systems, the large number of Soviet legacy or early Russian Federation systems led us to use replacement cost as a way to calculate the cost to Russia. Russia will replace each of these expended munitions in Table 3.5 with modern cruise and ballistic missiles, which currently are the Kh-101 ALCM, Iskander SRBM, Kalibr SLCM, P-800 ASCM, and perhaps a new anti-radiation missile. There is no official information on the cost of these missiles. Two separate sources suggest that the cost of Russia's Kalibr might be around $1 million, or 76 million rubles at the exchange rate we used for this report.[99] For comparison, the U.S. Navy spends $1.4 million per Tomahawk.[100] We have yet to uncover any credible estimates on the other Russian missiles.

Long-Range Precision Weapons Conclusion

As a preliminary estimate, we used the same replacement cost for all of Russia's expended missiles. This resulted in a total cost of 244.6 billion rubles, or $3.2 billion. Using the lower bound of 1,816 missiles, the replacement cost would be 138 billion rubles, or $1.8 billion. To replace 2,000 to 3,000 cruise and ballistic missiles might take Russia a decade, particularly if the higher-end expenditure estimate is more accurate. From 2016 to 2019, Russia reportedly produced 100 Kalibr missiles annually.[101] We did not have production estimates for other types of missiles.[102]

Conclusion

We estimated that Russia might have spent around 1.68 trillion rubles, or $22 billion over seven months of war to sustain primarily air and ground operations. When we added the cost of additional wartime pay (including one month of paying 300,000 mobilized reserves), the cost rose to 2.497 trillion rubles, or $33 billion. We estimated the materiel costs—the cost or replacement cost of lost weapons and the replacement cost of expended munitions—at 818 billion rubles, or $11 billion. Although it is not standard to aggregate flows (operational costs and compensation) with stocks (capital costs, specifically the cost of military materiel), any military budget will have both operating and capital costs, and doing such an aggregation is a fair way to estimate the overall cost of the war to Russia. That figure is 3.011 trillion rubles, or $39.6

---

[99] Solopov and Artem'ev, 2015; Myroslav Trinko, "Ukrainian Air Defense Forces Shot Down Two Kalibr Cruise Missiles Worth Almost $2,000,000 Fired from A Russian Submarine in the Black Sea," Gagadget.com, July 6, 2022.

[100] Mallory Shelbourne, "Raytheon Awarded $217M Tomahawk Missiles Contract for Navy, Marines, Army," *USNI News*, May 25, 2022.

[101] S. F. Vikulov (ed.), *Contemporary Issues in the Realization of the Military-Economic Potential of Russia in the First Quarter of the 21st Century and the Primary Areas for Military-Economic Research* [*Актуальные проблемы реализации веонно-экономического потенциала России в первой четверти XXI века и основные направления военно-экономических исследований*], Book 2, Kantsler, 2019.

[102] It is possible that Iran's drone sales to Russia, which occurred after the period of research for this study, could reduce Russia's replacement costs for precision munitions as the war continues.

billion (see Table 3.7). Because Russia has classified all such information related to defense spending, we were left to extrapolate from what little data were available to get a sense of the direct military costs to the Russian government. To put our estimated cost in perspective, Russia spent approximately 3.6 trillion rubles, or $47 billion on defense in all of 2021.[103]

Table 3.7. Estimated Total Direct Military Costs, February 24, 2022, to September 19, 2022

Domain	Cost (Billions of Rubles)	Cost (Billions of Dollars)
Air operations	193.2	2.5
Land operations	1,486.0	19.5
Regular combat, reserve, mercenary, and compensatory pay	513.9 [a]	6.7
Precision munition replacement cost	244.0	3.2
Replacement of weapons/equipment losses	574.0	7.5
Total	3,011.0	39.6

SOURCE: Authors' calculations using sources listed above.
[a] *Reserve pay* includes one month's average pay for 300,000 mobilized forces. Russia announced mobilization on September 21, 2022.

In this chapter, we attempted to provide some additional detail to the direct military losses and costs Russia has incurred as a result of this war. We examined some of the costs to maintain ground and air operations. We also explored what it might cost Russia to replace the large amounts of weaponry that were lost in the first six months of the war. Because so much information was unavailable, our findings are preliminary. By modern standards and by the standards of Russia's military today, losses of Russian lives and materiel have been substantial. Russia, by no means a rich country in comparison with its Western competitors and adversaries, in all likelihood is spending billions of dollars per month to maintain a war that as of late August 2022 appears as if it could go on for much longer. Russia will require years to return its military to the shape of 2021 in terms of professional personnel and modern weapons and equipment. And this is before the potentially costly and resisted occupation of seized portions of Ukraine.

---

[103] Ministry of Finance of the Russian Federation, 2022a.

Chapter 4. The Mechanisms of Russian Economic Decline

The sanctions placed on Russia put enormous pressure on the Russian economy. In some cases, the path of decline is clear: Russia will have less access to advanced technologies and to new technologies to be developed, and so will fade into a poorly performing, second-tier economy.[104] But in the shorter term, prospects were better than expected when the Western powers initially instituted sanctions. This chapter discusses the mechanisms by which Russia was outperforming expectations in the summer of 2022 and by which it was experiencing decline.

The Fundamental Problem Facing the Russian Economy

Largely because of export controls placed on Russia by the advanced Western countries, the Russian economy must undergo a fundamental transformation because it is losing access to inputs it uses in most of its industries. In the Bank of Russia's assessment, the financial sanctions were of less consequence than "restrictions on imports and logistics in foreign trade and, further on, with possible restrictions on Russian exports."[105] The sanctions caused "disruptions in technological, production and logistics chains."[106] As a result, Russian companies sought new markets and logistics routes, and the production of domestic components were increased or started from scratch. In addition, Russians in some cases were forced to cannibalize existing capital stock, such as by taking parts from existing Boeing and Airbus airplanes for installation in other Boeing and Airbus planes to ensure that they continue flying.[107] The Bank of Russia characterized this as "a period of structural transformation and the search for new business models for many enterprises."[108] The economic slowdown and the forced transformation of the Russian economy also resulted in the cancellation or ending of some investment projects.[109]

Outperformance of Expected Underperformance

Despite these threats to the Russian economy, negative economic performance started moderating in late spring 2022. By July, imports of consumer goods had improved because of

---

[104] Milanovic, 2022a.

[105] Bank of Russia, "Elvira Nabiullina's Speech at Joint Meeting of State Duma Dedicated Committees on Bank of Russia's 2021 Annual Report," April 18, 2022f.

[106] Bank of Russia, 2022g.

[107] "Exclusive: Russia Starts Stripping Jetliners for Parts as Sanctions Bite," Reuters, August 9, 2022.

[108] Bank of Russia, 2022f.

[109] Bank of Russia, 2022g.

new supply arrangements, but there still had been no recovery of imports of intermediate inputs and investment goods. Investment also remained muted because of economic uncertainty.[110]

The biggest reason that the Russian economy did not underperform as much as originally expected was because the sanctions did not block global energy exports, and oil prices have been high.[111] While export volumes were down, values rose dramatically (Table 4.1). In the first three months of 2022, Russian export revenues jumped to $166.4 billion, almost 60 percent higher than their value in the first three months of 2021. Likewise, in the second three months of 2022, they hit $153.1 billion, well above the mark of $127.9 billion in 2021. As of August 2022, there was strong evidence that most of the oil exports were being carried by Greek-owned tankers, enabled by insurance provided out of the United Kingdom, along with Norway and Sweden.[112] Major buyers included China, India, and the European Union (EU), despite the EU's many economic restrictions against Russia for the war.[113]

Table 4.1. Russia's Goods and Services Trade in Billions of Dollars

	2021		2022		Year-Over-Year Change (%)	
	Q1	Q2	Q1	Q2	Q1	Q2
Exports of goods and services	104.8	127.9	166.4	153.1	58.8	19.7
Imports of goods and services	79.1	93.2	88.7	72.3	12.1	-22.4
Trade balance	25.7	34.8	77.7	80.7	202.3	131.9

SOURCE: Bank of Russia, *Balance of Payments, Russian Federation* [Платежный Баланс, Российской Федерации], Vol. 11, Nos. 1–2, July 26, 2022p.
NOTE: Data for Q2 2022 are estimates. Q1 is January through March, and Q2 is April through June.

This higher export revenue proved to be a boost to the economy and the Russian federal budget. According to Russian Ministry of Finance data, federal budget revenues for the first half of 2022 amounted to 14.017 trillion rubles, compared with 11.266 trillion rubles the year

---

[110] Bank of Russia, "Statement by Bank of Russia Governor Elvira Nabiullina in Follow-Up to Board of Directors Meeting on 22 July 2022," July 22, 2022o.

[111] The price per barrel of benchmark Brent crude rose steadily from a low of $9.12 on April 21, 2020, to $99.29 on February 23, 2022. It then spiked to $127.52 by March 23, 2022, likely because of war-related precautionary buying and market adjustment, then fell again to $99.27 on April 5, 2022. It then rose steadily, peaking at $129.20 on June 8, before falling steadily, hitting a low of $76.02 on December 8, 2022 (U.S. Energy Information Administration, Europe Brent Spot Price FOB [Dollars per Barrel], data file, August 24, 2022, and December 29, 2022).

[112] Robin Brooks [@RobinBrooksIIF], "The insurance needed to operate these oil tankers is provided mainly out of the UK," Twitter post, August 24, 2022a; Robin Brooks [@RobinBrooksIIF], "We got many questions on this chart, which shows Greek oil tankers carrying the bulk of Russian oil," Twitter post, August 24, 2022b.

[113] Robert Perkins, "Russia's Seaborne Oil Exports Rise in August as Sanctions Impact Remains Muted," S&P Global Commodity Insights, August 18, 2022.

before.[114] Oil and gas revenue constituted 45.5 percent of total revenues in the 2022 period, compared with 33.5 percent in the 2021 period (Table 4.2).

Table 4.2. The Russian Federal Budget

	Billions of Rubles			Billions of U.S. Dollars		
	January–June 2021	January–June 2022	Difference	January–June 2021	January–June 2022	Difference
Revenues	11,265.8	14,016.8	2,751.1	148.2	184.4	36.2
Oil and gas revenues	3,776.0	6,375.9	2,599.9	49.7	83.9	34.2
Nonoil and gas revenues	7,489.8	7,640.9	151.1	98.5	100.5	2.0
Import related	2,212.7	1,926.9	−285.8	29.1	25.4	−3.8
Expenditures	10,491.1	12,642.9	2,151.8	138.0	166.4	28.3
Surplus or deficit	774.7	1,373.9	599.2	10.2	18.1	7.9
Nonoil surplus or deficit	−3,001.3	−5,002.1	−2,000.7	−39.5	−65.8	−26.3

SOURCE: Ministry of Finance of the Russian Federation, Federal Budget, spreadsheet, undated.
NOTE: Dollar values are calculated based on an exchange rate of 76 rubles to the dollar.

The inflows of resource revenues also meant that Russia's international reserves remained high, though about $300 billion worth were out of Russia's control because of sanctions.[115] In the week of February 21, 2022, just before the invasion, Russia valued its reserves at $639.6 billion. As late as August 26, 2022, it valued those reserves at $566.8 billion.[116] Furthermore, the central bank was able to lower its key interest rate, the rate the bank uses as a monetary policy tool, with the calming of inflationary pressures. By June 10, 2022, the bank had lowered the rate to 9.5 percent, the same level as just before the invasion, and by July 22, 2022, it had lowered the rate to 8.0 percent, the same level as the beginning of 2022 (Table 4.3).

---

[114] Ministry of Finance of the Russian Federation, undated.

[115] "Sanctions Have Frozen Around $300 Bln of Russian Reserves, FinMin Says," Reuters, March 13, 2022.

[116] Bank of Russia, International Reserves of the Russian Federation (End of Period), online data, last updated September 16, 2022r.

Table 4.3. Changes in the Bank of Russia Key Rate

Date	New Rate (%)	Increase (Basis Points)
February 11, 2022	9.5	+100
February 28, 2022	20.0	+1,050
April 8, 2022	17.0	−300
April 29, 2022	14.0	−300
May 26, 2022	11.0	−300
June 10, 2022	9.5	−150
July 22, 2022	8.0	−150

SOURCES: Bank of Russia, 2022b; Bank of Russia, "Bank of Russia Increases the Key Rate to 20% p.a.," press release, February 28, 2022c; Bank of Russia, "The Bank of Russia Cuts the Key Rate by 300 b.p. to 17.00% p.a.," press release, April 8, 2022e; Bank of Russia, "Bank of Russia Cuts the Key Rate by 300 b.p. to 14.00% p.a.," press release, April 29, 2022g; Bank of Russia, "Bank of Russia Cuts Key Rate by 300 bp to 11.00% p.a.," press release, May 26, 2022i; Bank of Russia, "Bank of Russia Cuts the Key Rate by 150 bp to 9.50% p.a.," press release, June 10, 2022j; Bank of Russia, "Bank of Russia Cuts the Key Rate by 150 b.p. to 8.00% p.a.," press release, July 22, 2022m.
NOTE: b.p. = basis points. One basis point = one one-hundredth of a percentage point. p.a. = per annum or per year.

Stresses on the Russian Economy

Despite the positive aspects of the economic track record of the first half of 2022, the Russian economy had many short-term problems and likely even more long-term problems. Although Russia found willing buyers for its oil and oil products, it had to endure a significant discount from world prices (Figure 4.1). Until January 2022, the price of Russian oil, known as Urals, closely tracked the standard European benchmark price of Brent crude. But in February, the prices started to diverge, and by April, Russia had to offer a discount of more than $30 per barrel.

Figure 4.1. The Price of Russian Oil Versus the International Benchmark

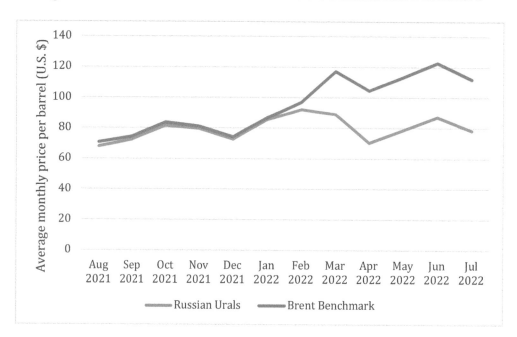

SOURCES: Statista Research Department, Average Monthly Price of Urals Crude Oil from January 2018 to July 2022 (in U.S. Dollars per Barrel), database, August 11, 2022a; U.S. Energy Information Administration, 2022.

Furthermore, even though federal revenues increased, federal expenditures also rose because of the cost of the war and additional social spending instituted in response to the war (Table 4.2). Federal spending for the first six months of 2022 amounted to 12.643 trillion rubles, 2.152 trillion rubles more than the same period in 2021, equivalent to $28.3 billion at an exchange rate of 76 rubles to the dollar. Furthermore, the ability to spend more appears to be driven entirely by oil and gas sales. Although there was a budget surplus of 1.374 trillion rubles for the first six months of 2022, the budget deficit based on revenues not stemming from oil and gas was 5.002 trillion. This was 2.001 trillion higher than the same period the previous year, or $26.3 billion.

This divergence between oil and gas revenues and other revenues, and the higher spending trends, were very clear in the July 2022 budget numbers, which were negative across several dimensions.[117] Oil and gas revenues fell 20 percent relative to the mark set in July 2021, whereas nonoil and gas revenues fell 30 percent. In contrast, total spending rose by 25 percent relative to spending in July 2021, and spending for January through July 2021 was up by more than 20 percent. Although hard data were not available, most of this growth likely was in defense and in domestic security and law enforcement, with modest increases in social support.[118]

An additional sign of economic decline is the fact that imports have been crushed. Imports in the second quarter of 2022, the first full quarter of the war, fell 22.4 percent relative to imports of

---

[117] "Russia's Federal Budget Sees Exceptional Drop in Revenues in July; Spending Continues to Rise," BOFIT Weekly 2022/33, The Bank of Finland Institute for Emerging Economies, August 19, 2022.

[118] "Russia's Federal Budget Sees Exceptional Drop in Revenues in July; Spending Continues to Rise," 2022.

goods and services in the second quarter of 2021 (Table 4.1).[119] This is the largest quarterly decline in imports since 2015—the year after Russia's first invasion of Ukraine and the start of Ukraine-related sanctions on Russia. Imports that year declined 34.3 percent in the first quarter relative to the same quarter in 2014, 37.4 percent in the second quarter, 35.7 percent in the third quarter, and 29.2 percent in the fourth quarter.[120] One notable difference was that the import declines of 2015 came with a collapse of oil prices. The average monthly spot price of Brent crude was $99 per barrel in 2014 and $52 per barrel in 2015.[121]

This decline can be seen in the indexes of industrial production (Table 4.4). The Russian industrial sector grew through the first quarter of 2022 relative to the first quarter of 2021, but then started shrinking. The decline took hold very quickly in manufacturing, with an index of 99.3 in March 2022, the first full month of the war, relative to March 2021. For January through July 2022, the hardest-hit sectors included manufacture of passenger cars, with an index of 35.8 relative to the same period in 2021; buses of not more than 5 tons gross vehicle weight at 58.1; and household refrigerators and freezers at 58.6. However, some sectors were above the level of 2021. Notably, these included some sectors targeted by Western export controls, suggesting some efforts at import substitution were succeeding, although likely with declines in quality. For the seven-month period, production of computers and their parts and accessories was at 137.6; production of semiconductor devices and parts was at 128.5; and radar equipment, radio navigation, and remote-control radio equipment was at 119.6.

---

[119] Data are in dollar terms from the Bank of Russia, and it is not clear what exchange rate was used.

[120] Bank of Russia, "Balance of Payments of the Russian Federation (in US$ Million), Standard Components [Платежный баланс Российской Федерации (в млн долларов США) Стандартные компоненты]," Excel spreadsheet, July 7, 2022l.

[121] U.S. Energy Information Administration, 2022.

Table 4.4. Industrial Production in 2022 Relative to the Same Month in 2021

Month	Overall	Mining	Manufacturing	Electricity, Gas, and Steam	Water Supply and Wastewater
January	108.0	107.8	110.0	101.1	99.7
February	105.4	107.4	106.2	95.2	104.8
March	102.3	106.6	99.3	101.4	108.3
April	97.4	97.2	97.0	102.1	92.5
May	97.6	97.8	96.5	104.3	95.8
June	97.6	101.4	95.3	99.8	84.3
July	99.5	100.9	98.9	99.5	85.1

SOURCE: Federal State Statistical Service (Rosstat), "About Industrial Production in January–July 2022 [О промышленном производстве в январе-июле 2022 года]," August 24, 2022e.
NOTE: "Electricity, gas, and steam" is more formally "Provision of electricity, gas and steam; air conditioning." "Water supply and wastewater" is more formally "Water supply; wastewater disposal, organization of and collection and disposal of waste, activities for elimination of pollution."

The decline in imports can also be seen in the budget numbers. While total revenues declined 25 percent in July 2022 relative to July 2021, revenues from value added taxes on imports fell by 40 percent, and revenues from tariffs on imports fell by about 60 percent.[122]

Other events also encouraged a trend toward further decline. Companies from advanced economies have been exiting Russia or curtailing operations. As of August 30, 2022, according to one estimate, 313 foreign companies had either halted their Russian operations or exited from Russia; 499 companies had temporarily stopped most or nearly all operations; 171 companies had scaled back significant business operations; and 159 companies had postponed future investment, development, or marketing while maintaining current operations.[123] In the short term, the consequences of the halted or reduced operations should be captured in the GDP estimates to the extent that they affect profits, wages, and taxes. But there are longer-term consequences. Foreign companies bring not only capital to their host country, but new methods and technologies, as well as global connections. These will be lost to Russia in the future.

With all these stresses, Russia is likely to receive in December 2022 its most significant shock since the early wave of sanctions. As part of its sixth sanctions package, the EU opted to end seaborne Russian oil imports by December 2022 and petroleum products by February 2023. Temporary exceptions were made for imports to selected countries.[124] In addition, as of

---

[122] "Russia's Federal Budget Sees Exceptional Drop in Revenues in July; Spending Continues to Rise," 2022.

[123] Chief Executive Leadership Institute, "Over 1,000 Companies Have Curtailed Operations in Russia—But Some Remain," updated by Jeffrey Sonnenfeld and Yale Research Team, Yale School of Management, Yale University, last updated August 30, 2022.

[124] European Commission, "Russia's War on Ukraine: EU Adopts Sixth Package of Sanctions Against Russia," press release, June 3, 2022.

December 2022, EU companies are no longer able to insure Russian seaborne oil cargos. This should result in Russian selling at an even deeper discount.

As of midsummer 2022, the EU was importing about 3 million barrels per day of Russian seaborne crude oil and products. Most of the imports of crude ended in December 2022 and of products in February 2023. In addition, Germany and Poland agreed to end imports of 500,000 barrels per day that come through the Druzhba pipeline.[125] Some of this will be directed elsewhere, and so, by one forecast, sales will fall by 1.2 million barrels per day.[126] At $80 per barrel, this would amount to a $35 billion decrease in annual revenue to Russia.[127]

Even without the EU action, there were other indications that Russia might not be able to maintain high oil revenues. In September 2022, India indicated that it would not purchase one of several particular blends from Russia—the East Siberia-Pacific Ocean (ESPO) blend—but instead would purchase from Africa and the Middle East because higher freight rates were making Russian oil uneconomical.[128] This particular blend constituted about 18 percent of total Indian purchases from Russia in July 2022. With freight charges, the Russian oil is reported to have been $5 to $7 more per barrel than Middle Eastern oil, and Middle Eastern oil has the added benefit of faster shipping time.

Russia benefited early in the war from higher oil prices and the ability to redirect oil sales. But, as with all other aspects of the Russian economy in wartime, the future is highly uncertain and the downside risks and trends far outweigh the upside possibilities.

---

[125] Perkins, 2022.

[126] Perkins, 2022.

[127] This estimate used the same price for crude oil and refined products. In 2021, the United States imported 48 million barrels of crude oil from Russia (harmonized tariff system code 2709) at an average price of $70.55 per barrel. That same year, the United States imported almost 190 million barrels of refined products (harmonized tariff system code 2710) at an average price of $69.66. However, almost 69 percent of the volume of the refined products was lower-value heavy fuel oil (harmonized tariff system code 2710.19.0635) at an average price of $67.05. Without that heavy fuel oil, the average value of refined products was $75.40 (U.S. International Trade Commission, Dataweb, online database, 2022).

[128] Nidhi Verma, "India Set to Skip Buying Russia's ESPO Crude in Sept as Freight Costs Jump," Reuters, September 22. 2022. The ESPO pipeline system and oil shipped through it is aimed at East Asian and U.S. West Coast markets (Mimansa Verma, "Days After Cautioning Putin on War, India May Skip Russian ESPO-Crude Oil Import," Quartz India, September 23, 2022).

Chapter 5. A Future of Likely Decline

As of late August 2022, Russia's intensified war on Ukraine has resulted in notable increases in defense expenditures, a broad decline of the Russian economy, and large-scale financial capital destruction. Economically, consequences have trended downward. GDP in every month starting in March 2022 was lower than GDP in the same month the year before (Table 5.1).

Table 5.1. Monthly GDP in 2022 Relative to the Same Period in 2021

Month	Change (%)
January	5.8
February	4.3
March	1.6
April	-2.8
May	-4.3
June	-5.0

SOURCES: "Russian GDP Growth Slows to 1.6% in March, Estimated at 3.7% in Q1—Econ Ministry," Interfax-Ukraine, April 28, 2022; "Crisis in Russian Economy Developing Along Flatter Trajectory, Signs of Stabilization Already Apparent—Central Bank," Interfax-Ukraine, July 12, 2022; "Big Differences Across Sectoral Contractions in Russia," BOFIT Weekly 2022/31, The Bank of Finland Institute for Emerging Economies, August 5, 2022.
NOTE: The June figure is reported as "nearly 5%" in "Big Differences Across Sectoral Contractions in Russia," 2022. No more-exact figure was available.

Military Losses and the Challenge of Rebuilding the Russian Armed Forces

In 2011, Russia embarked on ambitious military reforms to bring the armed forces into the 21st century. The central tenets of these reforms were professionalization and modernization. Russia made a strategic bet that highly trained soldiers equipped with modern weapons could replace the mass mobilization approach of the past. From 2011 to 2020, Russia recruited nearly 400,000 professional troops and planned to spend approximately 20 trillion rubles, or $263 billion to rearm the military with what were purported to be world-class weapons and command and control equipment.[129] The two primary tasks assigned to these new look forces was to dominate smaller militaries along the periphery in local wars and to deter a regional war with NATO through a mix of nuclear and strategic nonnuclear weapons—long-range precision munitions and strategic air defenses.

Russia's war in Ukraine will be a major setback for these reform efforts. Permanent readiness maneuver units—the motor rifle and tank BTGs—were a key pillar of Russia's plans to dominate

---

[129] Kofman and Lee, 2022; Anna Maria Dyner, *Assessment of the Russian Armed Forces' State Armament Programme in 2011-2020*, Polish Institute of International Affairs, June 2021.

the so-called near abroad. Losses of contract personnel and officers will take years to replace, particularly because Russia in recent years has struggled to increase the numbers of professional enlisted troops.[130] We have detailed Russian losses of modern tanks and IFVs, with the former eclipsing 1,000 in September 2022. Prior to the war, Russia was producing on average 140 T-72B3 MBTs.[131] Assuming a similar production rate going forward, it will take Russia about eight years to replace the tanks lost in Ukraine with models such as the T-72B3 or T-90M. IFV losses for Russia have been equally large and will probably have a similar replacement timeline, returning to the early 2022 order of battle as of the late 2020s. As the war has shown, without the ability to seize and hold territory, an artillery army alone does not buy much on the battlefield in any lasting sense.

Russia will experience similar lags in rebuilding the central offensive component of its planned force posture for regional warfighting—its long-range conventional strike complex. We should recall that the disposition of Russian forces and the bulk of NATO military potential is such that each side needs long-range firepower to push back or slow down the other side. In the decade prior to the war in Ukraine, Russia was slowly building up long-range precision munition stockpiles that were mostly earmarked for a regional war in Europe until a larger inventory could be established.[132] One Russian source stated that Russian production of the Kalibr family of cruise missiles was 100 per year from 2016 to 2019.[133] As we noted earlier, Russia reportedly has launched over 3,000 guided munitions in seven months of war. Assuming a production rate of 100 per year for the three primary missiles of the nonnuclear *triad*—the Kh-101 conventional ALCM, the Iskander SRBM, and the Kalibr SLCM—it would take Russia until 2032 to return to the level of a decade prior. This will have significant implications for Russian regional deterrence and warfighting throughout the 2020s.

Near-Term Ramifications

In the near term, even as losses and costs for Russia mount, there is little indication that they will drive Russia to end its war effort. While sanctions reportedly froze about $300 billion in Russian reserves, total reserves as of the end of August were $566.8 billion, meaning Russia had about $266.8 billion to use, about seven-and-a-half times our estimate of the direct military costs of the first seven months of the war. In addition, as of the beginning of February, Russia reported

---

[130] Alexei Savelov, "The Number of Military Servicemembers on Contract in the Russian Military Has More Than Doubled [Численность военнослужащих по контракту в российской армии возросла более чем в два раза]," *Tvzvezda*, June 11, 2018; Ministry of Defense, presentation, 2012-2020. Note that in the first source from 2018 and the second from 2020 the number of contract soldiers remained unchanged.

[131] International Institute for Strategic Studies, *The Military Balance 2020*, 1st ed., Routledge, 2020.

[132] Westerlund et al., 2019.

[133] Vikulov, 2019.

a value of $174.9 billion for the National Wealth Fund.[134] Along with many other entities, the National Wealth Fund was sanctioned early in the war, but it is not clear how much of the fund this action froze.[135] The fund held liquid assets in euros, British pounds, Japanese yen, Chinese renminbi, and rubles; gold; and nonliquid, mostly ruble assets in the form of infrastructure investments, bank deposits, and other instruments.[136] A rough estimate is that the fund's assets were about 55 percent foreign-currency denominated, including renminbi, 32 percent ruble denominated, and 13 percent gold at February 1, 2022, exchange rates and prices.[137] While the liquid foreign currency assets and gold are included in Russia's total international reserves, it is not clear how many of these foreign-currency denominated assets could be blocked by sanctioning countries. What is clear is that Russia has been spending from the fund to support the economy. It spent a reported 535 billion rubles ($7 billion) to support financial stability through September 2022, with money going to Russian Railways, Aeroflot, Gazprombank, and a state-owned housing finance entity, among others.[138] And if these sources of funding prove inadequate, Russia can always finance its wartime activities as a last resort by printing money—a practice employed by states when domestic support for a war is low.[139] The decline of the Russian economy and increasing costs of the war might drive Russia to cut its domestic expenditures, but that is more likely to occur over an unspecified medium term rather than in 2022, and it is unlikely to cause the war effort to be suspended even in the medium term.

Long-Term Economic Decline

Just as the outlook for war spending is negative, the outlook for the economy is negative. Although both the Bank of Russia and the Ministry of Economic Development project that annual GDP change will be positive in 2024, there is enormous uncertainty of which they cannot take account, even with the most-refined models. And with sanctions likely to remain for years, if not decades, Russia is likely to fall well behind the world in technological development.

The saving grace for Russia as of late summer was revenues from oil and gas exports. Those have enabled Russia to fund its war effort, imports, and social spending to maintain some degree of normal life among the population. Most oil exports to the EU are to end by early 2024, but reducing them to the rest of the world might be a challenge. The late-September 2022 decision

---

[134] Ministry of Finance of the Russian Federation, "Volume of the National Wealth Fund," February 24, 2022b.

[135] U.S. Department of the Treasury, 2022c.

[136] Charles Lichfield, *Windfall: How Russia Managed Oil and Gas Income After Invading Ukraine, and How It Will Have to Make Do with Less*, Atlantic Council, November 30, 2022.

[137] Exchange rate data are from "Exchange Rates United Kingdom," webpage, 2022. Gold price is from GoldPrice, homepage, 2022.

[138] Elena Fabrichnaya and Alexander Marrow, "Russia to Spend $6.8 Billion From Wealth Fund on Infrastructure Projects in 2022," Reuters, September 23, 2022.

[139] Rosella Cappella, *The Political Economy of War Finance*, dissertation, University of Pennsylvania, 2012.

by Indian importers not to buy the Russian ESPO blend shows that even if international sales are possible, Russia will be under tremendous pressure to provide discounted prices. The West's ability to close off Russia's oil economy is the largest uncertainty regarding the sustainability of Russia's war effort and the path of its economy, but it is also the most powerful lever for ending the war on terms favorable to Ukraine and the West.

The Future of the Russian Threat

This report suggests that Putin's war on Ukraine will push Russia into a window of weakness over the next decade. Russia will retain its nuclear potential, to be sure, and the losses in conventional firepower mean that a desperate or threatened Russia could resort to nuclear use more quickly in crisis. Short of that extreme scenario, however, Russia's military will endure shortfalls in the years to come in some of the key tools of local and regional warfighting. Newly recruited contract soldiers will require years to catch up to their fallen comrades in training and expertise. Russia will also have less access to the Western technology it relies on to modernize the armed forces. There is also the cost of occupation and potentially making these territories a part of the Russian Federation, in terms of both budget resources and management from the Kremlin and its ministries. Once a country gets bogged down with one adversary, it becomes increasingly difficult to maintain stability at home and to pursue disparate interests elsewhere around the globe. Ukraine will be a drain on the Russian military and economy for the foreseeable future, and the end result could ultimately be catastrophic for the Putin regime.

Weakness is a relative term, however. The current cohesion of the Western alliance, which as of April 2023 added Finland to NATO and was expected to add Sweden as well, makes Russia look weak by comparison with traditional state power indicators. A divided Europe or a more reclusive United States could change the power dynamic even as Russia struggles to crawl out of the hole into which it has dug itself in Ukraine. A war in the Pacific that leads to direct U.S. military involvement could also be a boon to Russian actions along its western border. Friendly Russian relations with China and India could also help to soften the blow over the next decade, although Russia's weakened position will not help its negotiating position for access to these markets or their expertise in areas of interest.

While the Russian threat will evolve, the war on Ukraine is unlikely to come to a quick end due only to its consequences on the Russian economy and military. Even though the Russian economy faces near-term and long-term impairment because of sanctions and other structural factors, and war operations are proving expensive, we judge these costs to be sustainable for the next several years. War costs alone will not cause Russia to end its Ukraine invasion. More likely, a combination of battlefield losses, economic decline, a drop in living standards, social unrest, and elite dissatisfaction will be among the driving forces behind any potential change in Russia's war effort.

Chapter 6. Postscript: The Costs of War by Late Summer 2023

Work for this report was completed in late summer 2022; modest updates were made through December 2022. DAF cleared this report for public release on September 13, 2023. To account for this publication delay, this postscript includes brief updates using the same methods used for the original report.

The costs detailed in Chapters 1 through 5 continued to mount. Sanctions and export controls have also taken a toll on the economy.[140]

We estimated that the war caused Russia GDP losses of between $81 billion and $104 billion in 2022. Regarding direct military spending, we estimated Russia is poised to spend a minimum of $131.6 billion (10 trillion rubles) on the war from early 2022 through 2024. We further estimated that $47.4 billion of that would be spent in 2022 and 2023.[141] That figure could be higher after taking into account administrative costs in the occupied territories, the longer-term costs of replacing weapons, and the costs of managing the care of veterans.

Despite these costs and prospective costs, the economy started to rebound in 2023; GDP growth was expected to be positive in 2023, and some of the direr costs were moderated. In large part, this was because of sizable government spending, but it was also because of more-general adjustment efforts on the part of businesses, consumers, and the government. Moreover, because of mobilization, Russia is already in the process of reconstituting its military and is reportedly ramping up production because its industry has not suffered from physical attacks during the war. For example, Russia has doubled the annual output of tanks to 200 from 100 in the prewar environment.[142] Russia could therefore have a sizable, if low-tech, land force when the war ends. If it manages to maintain elevated production levels of key land warfare systems in the postwar period, by 2030 or 2035 Russia could further expand and modernize its military (with the necessary caveats about the competent employment of this force, Russia's ability to obtain the requisite components, and its ability to sustain the resource allocation for the reconstitution of its defense capability).

---

[140] For a detailed review on the costs of sanctions, export controls, and other economic restrictions, see Yulia Bychkovska, Ana Mikadze, and Jacob Saionz, *Working Hard or Hardly Working? Understanding the Sanctions' Effects on Russia's Economy and War Effort*, Maxwell School at Syracuse University, June 20, 2023.

[141] In Table 6.6 later in this section, we subtract notional defense spending if the war had not occurred from estimates and projections of what Russia will have spent on defense from 2022 to 2024 to arrive at this figure of 10 trillion rubles for the war.

[142] Julian E. Barnes, Eric Schmitt, and Thomas Gibbons-Neff, "Russia Overcomes Sanctions to Expand Missile Production, Officials Say," *New York Times*, September 13, 2023.

In this postscript, we retain the use of a constant conversion rate of 76 rubles to the dollar given Russia's restricted capital account.[143] Recorded ruble exchange rates have been volatile and, in fall 2022, started a steady depreciation, reaching a monthly average of the daily rate of 90.4 rubles to the dollar in July 2023 (Figure 6.1).

Figure 6.1. Monthly Average of the Daily Ruble-Dollar Exchange Rate

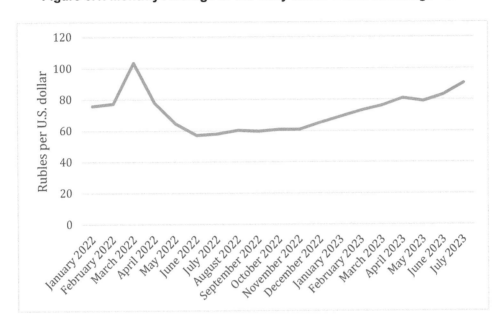

SOURCE: Drawn using information from Organization for Economic Co-operation and Development, 2022.

Overall Costs

The war has badly affected the Russian economy, turning 2022 from a year that might have had positive growth into a year that had negative growth. In this section, we review GDP, financial capital destruction, and changes in human capital. In the next section, we review underlying economic activity, specifically trade, industrial production, and oil prices.

GDP

We start with the consequences for the full year of 2022 and then consider the first half of 2023. To consider the effect on GDP, we compared projected 2022 real GDP growth just before the war began with actual 2022 real GDP growth (Table 6.1). Both Rosstat, Russia's statistical

---

[143] See, for example, Bank of Russia, "Bank of Russia Extends Restrictions for Non-Residents from Unfriendly Countries to Transfer Money Abroad from Brokerage and Trust Management Accounts," press release, September 26, 2023j; Bank of Russia, "Bank of Russia Extends Restrictions on Money Transfers Abroad for Another Six Months," press release, September 29, 2023k.

agency, and the International Monetary Fund, reported a decline of 2.1 percent for 2022 real GDP.[144] This is much different from projections before the start of the war.

Table 6.1. Projected 2022 GDP Growth Before Russia's Invasion of Ukraine

Organization	Forecast (%)	Date of Forecast
World Bank	2.4	January 2022
International Monetary Fund	2.8	January 2022
Bank of Russia	2.0–3.0	February 11, 2022

SOURCES: World Bank, *Global Economic Prospects*, January 2022a; International Monetary Fund, *World Economic Outlook Update: Rising Caseloads, a Disrupted Recovery, and Higher Inflation*, January 2022a; Bank of Russia, 2022b.

Using the figures from the Bank of Russia (because they bracket the World Bank and International Monetary Fund figures), real GDP grew between 4.1 percentage points and 5.1 percentage points less than expected. Not all of this can be credited to the war, but it is not clear whether any other major events in 2022 would have changed Russia's economic trajectory.

To calculate the economic loss, we followed the same method we used in Chapter 2; specifically, we applied the percentage-point gap to 2021 nominal GDP and then, because the growth gap is in real terms, applied an inflation factor to calculate a nominal result. We show this in Table 6.2. Table 6.2 repeats Table 2.1 except with the addition of three new lines that show the inflation-adjusted figures.[145] Using this method results in a nominal loss of between $81 billion and $104 billion dollars in 2022.

---

[144] Federal State Statistical Service (Rosstat), "On the Production and Use of Gross Domestic Product (GDP) in 2022 [О производстве и использовании валового внутреннего продукта (ВВП) в 2022 году]," April 7, 2023a; International Monetary Fund, *World Economic Outlook Update: Near-Term Resilience, Persistent Challenges*, July 2023.

[145] Annual inflation in 2022 was 14.5 percent. See Bank of Russia, *Monetary Policy Report, February 2023*, No. 1, February 20, 2023a, p. 5.

Table 6.2. Revised Projected Russian GDP Loss, 2022

Projection Description	Low	High
2022 GDP change, Bank of Russia January projection (%)	2.0	3.0
2022 actual GDP change (%)	–2.1	–2.1
Total projected change from prewar projections (%)	–4.1	–5.0
Lost GDP		
U.S. dollar terms (billion, real)	73	91
Ruble terms (billion, real)	5,363	6,671
U.S. dollar terms with ruble terms converted at 76 rubles per dollar (billion, real)	71	88
U.S. dollar terms (billion, nominal)	83	104
Ruble terms (billion, nominal)	6,140	7,638
U.S. dollar terms with ruble terms converted at 76 rubles per dollar (billion, nominal)	81	100
Addendum: 2021 Nominal Russian GDP		
U.S. dollars (billion)	1,775.8	
Russian rubles (billion)	130,795.3	

SOURCES: Bank of Russia, 2022b; Bank of Russia, 2022n; World Bank, 2022b.
NOTE: Projected GDP changes are in real terms. The U.S. dollar estimate for lost GDP uses the dollar figure for 2021 nominal GDP from the World Bank's World Development Indicators. The ruble estimate uses the ruble figure for 2021 nominal GDP from the same source. The second estimate in U.S. dollar terms converts ruble losses at the rate of 76 rubles to the dollar (as explained in Chapter 1).

Another way to consider the decline is to consider GDP in the fourth quarter of 2022 relative to GDP in the fourth quarter of 2021. On this basis, real GDP declined by 2.7 percent.[146] This would make the gap in real GDP growth on the order of 4.7 percentage points to 5.7 percentage points. A very rough calculation along the lines of the preceding calculation would then show total real GDP losses of $83 billion to $101 billion and nominal GDP losses of $96 billion to $116 billion.[147]

This is far less than early predictions when the war started. One major reason for the better-than-expected performance was public spending. In the words of Bank of Russia Governor Elvira Nabiullina, "Public spending and public demand have had a significant impact, especially last year. At the time, there was a drop in private demand, which was essentially replaced by public demand."[148] This can be seen in the official budget numbers. Federal budget expenditures

---

[146] Bank of Russia "Bank of Russia's Medium-Term Forecast Following the Bank of Russia Board of Directors' Key Rate Meeting on 15 September 2023," press release, September 15, 2023h.

[147] This calculation depends on Russia's end-of-year 2021 real GDP being similar to its full-year 2021 real GDP. Given growth throughout 2021, these figures likely are an overestimation and thus provide an upper bound.

[148] Bank of Russia, "Statement by Bank of Russia Governor Elvira Nabiullina in Follow-Up to Board of Directors Meeting on 21 July 2023," Speech, July 21, 2023c.

rose from 24.8 trillion rubles in 2021 to 31.1 trillion rubles in 2022, and the non-oil deficit nearly doubled from 8.5 trillion rubles in 2021 to 14.9 trillion rubles in 2022.[149]

According to official statistics, real GDP continued to decline in the beginning of 2023; first quarter real 2023 GDP was 1.8 percent below that of 2022 first quarter real GDP.[150] However, growth returned by the second quarter; real second quarter 2023 GDP was up 4.9 percent relative to second quarter real 2022 GDP.[151] Real 2023 GDP for the first half of the year was up 1.6 percent relative to the same period a year earlier.

Before the war, the Bank of Russia projected that 2023 GDP would rise by 1.5 percent to 2.5 percent above 2022 GDP.[152] If 2023 growth were to remain on the same trajectory in the second half of 2023 as in the first half, then total GDP growth for the year would be at the low end of the prewar forecast. This means that in 2023, Russia would not have continued to lose income because of the war, but it also means that Russia would not have made up for 2022 losses. If the sanctions, export controls, and Russia's own inefficiencies in adjusting to a wartime economy continue, then the loss in 2022 could be permanent.

One other way to look at Russia's loss of income is to consider seasonally adjusted quarterly real GDP.[153] This figure grew every quarter from the previous quarter (not the year-ago-quarter) from the first quarter of 2016 through the third quarter of 2019. It then fell through the COVID-19 pandemic but then rose again every quarter from the third quarter of 2020 through the first quarter of 2022. Although it rose in several quarters since then, as of the second quarter of 2023 it remained below the levels hit in the third and fourth quarters of 2021 and the first quarter of 2022, indicating a significant loss of income for Russia. In the second quarter of 2023, it registered 33,728 billion rubles on a quarterly basis, below the first-quarter 2022 figure of 34,203 billion rubles.

Financial Capital Destruction

By the end of 2022, the total market capitalization of the Moscow Exchange had stabilized and risen below its third-quarter 2022 trough (Table 6.3). This increase continued through the first half of 2023, and market capitalization returned to about its level at the end of the first quarter of 2022, the first quarter in which Russia's full-scale invasion was active (Table 2.3).

---

[149] Ministry of Finance of the Russian Federation, "Federal Budget," spreadsheet, September 21, 2023d.

[150] Federal State Statistical Service (Rosstat), "On Production of Gross Domestic Product in the First Quarter of 2023" [О ПРОИЗВОДСТВЕ ВАЛОВОГО ВНУТРЕННЕГО ПРОДУКТА В I КВАРТАЛЕ 2023 ГОДА], Moscow, June 15, 2023b. These figures are not seasonally adjusted.

[151] Federal State Statistical Service (Rosstat), "On Production of Gross Domestic Product in the First Quarter of 2023" [О ПРОИЗВОДСТВЕ ВАЛОВОГО ВНУТРЕННЕГО ПРОДУКТА В II КВАРТАЛЕ 2023 ГОДА], Moscow, September 8, 2023e. These figures are not seasonally adjusted.

[152] Bank of Russia, 2022b.

[153] Federal State Statistical Service (Rosstat), "GDP Quarters (Since 1995) [ВВП кварталы (с 1995 г.)]," spreadsheet, August 9, 2023d.

However, even by June 2023, market capitalization was still more than 24 percent below its prewar peak, reached at the end of September 2021. This equals a total financial capital destruction of 15.92 trillion rubles, or $209.5 billion.

Table 6.3. Market Capitalization of the Moscow Exchange Equities Market

Date	Value in Rubles (trillion)	Value in Dollars (billion)
September 30, 2022	33.75	444
December 31, 2022	38.40	505
March 31, 2023	43.44	572
June 30, 2023	49.13	646

SOURCES: Moscow Exchange, 2022f; Moscow Exchange, "Moscow Exchange Announces Results for the Full Year 2022," press release, March 10, 2023a; Moscow Exchange, "Moscow Exchange Announces Results for the First Quarter of 2023," press release, May 22, 2023b; Moscow Exchange, "Moscow Exchange Announces Results for the second Quarter of 2023," press release, August 23, 2023c.
NOTE: The Moscow Exchange press releases provide different dollar amounts than those listed in the table. As explained in the main text, we converted all ruble amounts at the rate of 76 to the dollar. The amounts given by the Moscow Exchange are as follows (all in billions of U.S. dollars): Q3 2022, $588; Q4 2022, $530; Q1 2023, $557; and Q2 2023, $565.

Human Capital Destruction

As discussed in Chapter 2, human capital destruction occurs because working-age people are killed or wounded in the war, because their participation in the war limits their training and education or on-the-job experience, or because people have left Russia.

An estimate in late July 2023, drawing on data from receiving countries, put the number of people who have left Russia at between 817,000 and 922,000. The analysis about that estimate further noted that "this outflow amounts to approximately 1% of Russia's labour force and is characterised by a notable concentration of individuals with higher income levels and significant social capital."[154] Other sources noted that this emigration has included more than a fifth of Russia's "top programmers," "highly skilled doctors," and "skilled workers."[155]

A separate analysis in August 2023 noted a variety of ways beyond emigration that the war is hurting Russia's human capital. It said that about 5 percent of Russian men between ages 20 and 40 have either emigrated or been drafted in the armed forces. One estimate it cited was that 40,000 to 60,000 people have been killed. Furthermore, emigration and service in the war has lowered the birthrate, hurting future human capital development.[156]

---

[154] Re: Russia, "Escape from War: New Data Puts the Number of Russians Who Have Left at More than 800,000," *Review*, July 2023. *The Economist* appears to find this work credible and cites it extensively in "Russians Have Emigrated in Huge Numbers Since the War in Ukraine," *The Economist*, August 23, 2023.

[155] "Putin Orders Measures to Reverse Mass Wartime Exodus," *Moscow Times*, May 12, 2023.

[156] Bat Chen Druyan Feldman and Arkady Mil-Man, "The War in Ukraine: Exacerbating Russia's Demographic Crisis," Institute for National Security Studies, August 22, 2023.

A reduction of between 1 percent and 5 percent of working-age people can have negative consequences for the economy, though the exact connection to Russia's economic performance is not clear. Such skilled workers as programmers can continue to work for Russian enterprises remotely. However, as of late summer 2023, Russia was experiencing a tight labor market, which the Bank of Russia noted was caused largely by the expansion of government spending and the expansion of Russian businesses producing substitutes for items that were no longer imported.[157] In an August 2023 survey, 60 percent of businesses reported having hiring difficulties, especially of specialists. This was especially true in manufacturing and, within manufacturing, in machine building, chemicals, and metallurgy. Meanwhile, with labor demand rising rapidly, supply in the first half of 2023 relative to the first half of 2022 rose by 100,000 people, about 0.1 percent of total labor supply.[158]

Emigration does appear to be a concern to Russian leadership. In May 2023, Putin issued a decree for the government to develop measures to reverse emigration, one goal of which was to "preserve human capital."[159]

Underlying Patterns in the Russian Economy

Underlying the overall trends in income losses, financial capital destruction, and human capital destruction is a variety of business activities. Extending the information in Chapter 4, we focused on trade, industrial production, and oil prices. In each case, activity started to return to normal in 2023 but with remaining weaknesses.

Signs of this return to more normal activity are inflation and the key interest rate. In July 2023, the Bank of Russia reported that domestic demand was exceeding domestic capacity to expand production, exacerbated by labor shortages and ruble depreciation, reinforcing inflation; inflation expectations had also risen.[160] In 2022, the Bank of Russia's last interest rate cut came in September 2022, when it cut the rate to 7.5 percent (see Table 4.3).[161] It maintained that rate until July 2023, when it raised the rate to 8.5 percent, then 12 percent in August 2023, and then 13 percent in September 2023.[162]

---

[157] Bank of Russia, *Regional Economy: Commentaries by Bank of Russia Main Branches*, No. 22, September 6, 2023f.

[158] Bank of Russia, 2023f, pp. 24–25.

[159] "Putin Orders Measures to Reverse Mass Wartime Exodus," *The Moscow Times*, May 12, 2023.

[160] Bank of Russia, "Bank of Russia Increases Key Rate by 100 b.p. to 8.50% p.a.," press release, July 21, 2023b.

[161] Bank of Russia, "Bank of Russia Cuts Key Rate by 50 b.p. to 7.50% p.a.," press release, September 16, 2022q.

[162] Bank of Russia, 2023b; Bank of Russia, "Bank of Russia Increases Key Rate by 350 b.p. to 12.50% p.a.," press release, August 15, 2023e; Bank of Russia, "Bank of Russia Increases Key Rate by 100 b.p. to 13.00% p.a.," press release, September 15, 2023g.

Trade

During the first part of the war, Russia's exports expanded thanks to high oil prices, but its imports contracted because of sanctions and economic disruption. By 2023, the situation had reversed; exports were down significantly because of sanctions and slowing world growth, and imports were back to where they had been before February 2022 (Table 6.4). As with GDP, imports were boosted by higher government spending and growth in lending.[163]

Table 6.4. Russia's Goods and Services Trade, Billion U.S. Dollars

Period	Exports	Imports
2021 Q1	104.8	79.1
2021 Q2	127.9	93.2
2021 Q3	146.2	98.9
2021 Q4	171.0	108.8
2022 Q1	168.4	87.3
2022 Q2	162.9	71.5
2022 Q3	152.7	87.1
2022 Q4	155.4	101.9
2023 Q1	114.3	91.6
2023 Q2	110.7	95.1

SOURCE: Bank of Russia, *Russia's Balance of Payments, Information and Analytical Commentary,* No. 2, Vol. 15, July 25, 2023d.
NOTE: Figures may differ from those of Table 4.1 because of data revisions.

Industrial Production

The index of industrial production in Russia continued to decline most months through February 2023 (Table 6.5). However, in line with the economy, it picked back up by spring 2023. It also helped that the 2023 figures were relative to the low base of 2022 and would more easily be boosted by increased government spending.

---

[163] Bank of Russia, "Statement by Bank of Russia Governor Elvira Nabiullina in Follow-Up to Board of Directors Meeting on 15 September 2023," press release, September 15, 2023i.

Table 6.5. Industrial Production Relative to the Same Month in the Previous Year

Month	Index
July 2022	100.5
August 2022	100.7
September 2022	98.0
October 2022	98.4
November 2022	99.6
December 2022	97.9
January 2023	97.1
February 2023	98.3
March 2023	100.9
April 2023	104.9
May 2023	106.7
June 2023	105.8
July 2023	104.9
August 2023	105.4

SOURCE: Federal State Statistical Service (Rosstat), "About Industrial Production in January–August 2023 [О промышленном производстве в Январе–Августе 2023 года]," September 27, 2023f.
NOTE: The July 2022 figure differs from that of Table 4.4 because of data revisions.

Oil Price

Oil and gas revenues remained important to the Russian federal budget. Between January 2022 and August 2022, they constituted 44.4 percent of federal budget revenues. However, for the same period in 2023, they constituted only 28.4 percent.[164]

After increases in February, March, and April 2022, the monthly average price per barrel of Russia's benchmark Urals crude oil fell through March 2023 (Figure 6.2). Even with increases since then, it is well below the highs of spring and summer 2022. Furthermore, it has remained at a discount to the benchmark Brent crude selling price, though that discount has narrowed (Figure 6.2 and Figure 6.3). This has resulted in lower export revenues for Russia and lower oil and gas revenues for the budget.

---

[164] Federal State Statistical Service (Rosstat), 2023d.

Figure 6.2. The Price of Russian Oil Versus the International Benchmark

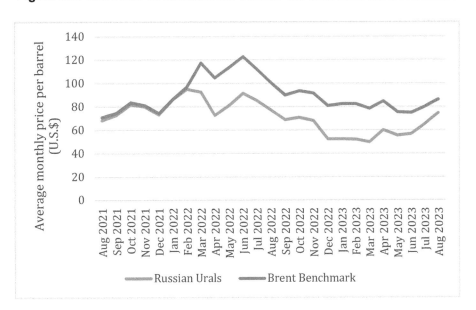

SOURCES: Statista Research Department, "Average Monthly Price of Urals Crude Oil from January 2007 to August 2023," dataset, September 13, 2023; U.S. Energy Information Administration, "Europe Brent Spot Price FOB (Dollars per Barrel)," dataset, September 27, 2023.

Figure 6.3. The Price Discount for Russian Oil

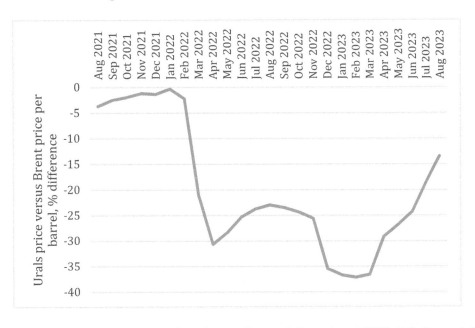

SOURCES: Statista Research Department, 2022b; Statista Research Department, 2023; U.S. Energy Information Administration, 2023.

Direct Military Costs

When we initially reported on direct military costs to Russia of its war on Ukraine, there was a dearth of official information, and the war had been ongoing for a short time. The picture has marginally improved as of October 2023; informed analysts are producing estimates of Russian defense spending in 2022, and the Russian government has released defense spending estimates for 2023 and 2024 that offer a better, though still incomplete, sense of the cost of the war. Drawing on data from the Moscow-based Gaidar Institute, the Russia defense economics expert Julian Cooper estimated that Russia spent 5.1 trillion rubles on defense in 2022.[165] Russian official reporting from the Ministry of Finance showed that Russia in 2021 spent approximately 3.5 trillion rubles on defense. Had Russia increased defense spending by 8 percent and not launched the war, it would have spent 3.8 trillion rubles on defense as opposed to 5.1 trillion. Thus, we assume Russia spent at least an extra 1.3 trillion rubles in 2022 because of the war (we assume some war-related spending is not accounted for in the defense spending line item; see below).

In our initial research from mid-2022, we used a small, three-month sample of official spending data from early 2022 to estimate 1.6 trillion rubles for seven months of war. This figure rose to more than 3 trillion rubles when we factored in other costs, such as combat pay and replacement costs for weapons and high-end long-range precision munitions. One way to account for the large difference in the two estimates—3 trillion for seven months of war versus 1.3 trillion for 10 months of war—is that, for much of 2022, the Russian budget might not yet have reflected the full effects of increased combat pay and replacement costs for weapons and personnel losses, requirements that became much more acute toward the end of 2022 and into 2023 as the war bogged down into an attritional struggle (see Table 6.6, which shows how Russian weapons losses have doubled since we finished our initial research). These costs are probably better reflected in projections of higher Russian defense spending estimates for 2023 and 2024.

Table 6.6. Selected Russian Weapons Losses, September 2022 Through September 2023

Type	Losses as of September 2022	Losses as of September 2023
Main Battle Tank	1,155	2,349
AFV	600	988
IFV	1,280	2,834
APC	162	355
SPA	206	544
MRL	109	280
Total	3,512	7,350

SOURCE: Jakub Janovsky, naalsio26, Aloha, Dan, and Kemal, "Attack on Europe: Documenting Russian Equipment Losses During the Russian Invasion of Ukraine," Oryx, February 24, 2022.

---

[165] Julian Cooper, *Russia's Military Expenditure During Its War Against Ukraine*, Stockholm International Peace Research Institute, June 2023, p. 5.

Russia's Ministry of Finance has reported that Russia will spend approximately 6.4 trillion rubles in 2023 on defense and close to 10.8 trillion rubles in 2024.[166] This amount of 10.8 trillion rubles is more than three times what Russia spent on prewar defense in 2021. So, the current and future cost of the war, which is more in line with our initial estimates that took into account the cost of not only conducting operations but replacing losses of materiel and increased pay and compensation, is rising dramatically for Russia as the war drags on (Table 6.7).

Table 6.7. The Minimum Direct Cost of Russia's War on Ukraine, 2022–2024 (trillion rubles)

Spending Category	2022	2023	2024	Total
Defense spending (actual and projected)	5.1	6.4	10.8	22.3
Notional defense spending without the war[a]	3.8	4.1	4.4	12.3
Cost of war (minimum)	1.3	2.3	6.4	10.0

SOURCE: Ministry of Finance of the Russian Federation, 2023d.
[a] Assumes an 8-percent growth rate in defense spending year over year from a starting point of 3.5 trillion rubles in 2021.

Not captured in our initial research was increased pay for industry, a portion of which is reportedly working around the clock. There is evidence that Russian enterprises are now offering double or triple prewar salaries to recruit new hires to keep up with demand.[167] Furthermore, there are additional costs that probably are not captured in the national defense spending line item in the Russian budget. A significant one could be the cost of administration of the newly occupied territories in Ukraine, where approximately 1.5 million people reside.

Conclusion

We estimate that the war caused GDP losses of between $81 billion and $104 billion in 2022. Direct military spending is likely to total a cumulative $47.4 billion through the end of 2023 and a cumulative $131.6 billion through the end of 2024.

Direct military costs for Russia are rising substantially as the war progresses well into its second year. This is because Russia had to mobilize and equip hundreds of thousands more troops, and it is having to replace substantial weapons and equipment losses. Russia is also reportedly having to raise pay for service in a combat zone and in industry to recruit workers to meet the Ministry of Defense's demand. In our initial assessment, we tried to consider such

---

[166] Darya Korsunskaya and Alexander Marrow, "'Everything for the Front': Russia Allots a Third of 2024 Spending to Defence," *Reuters*, October 2, 2023.

[167] Department of Employment of the Amur Region [Управление занятости населения Амурской области / Upravlenie zaniatosti naseleniia Amurskoi oblasti], Vkontakte, webpage, November 16, 2022.

costs. This probably exaggerated the cost for Russia as of mid-2022. As time has gone on, however, these replacement and additional costs appear to now be finding their way into official Russian budget projections for 2023 and 2024, which are more in line with our estimates in August 2022.

Despite the soaring costs, Russia can weather the storm by running deficits and funding them by borrowing or drawing from its National Welfare Fund. However, there are limits to support from the National Welfare Fund. As of September 2023, its total value was 13.7 trillion rubles, which the Ministry of Finance valued at 9.1 percent of GDP.[168] Note that this is well below projected 2023 and 2024 defense spending. In addition, some of these assets might be frozen in the West. Others are illiquid, allocated as capital contributions to VEB.RF or as loans to businesses via VEB.RF.[169]

Russia does have other sources of money to finance the war. It retains borrowing capacity, with a low debt to GDP ratio.[170] It can raise taxes. And, if necessary, it can cut spending in non-defense budget lines. Accordingly, even though the war is costly, it remains the case that Russia has the financial wherewithal to continue to conduct it for at least several more years.

---

[168] Ministry of Finance of the Russian Federation, "Volume of the National Wealth Fund," September 12, 2023c.

[169] Ministry of Finance of the Russian Federation, "Allocation of the National Wealth Fund's Assets to Deposits in VEB.RF," September 9, 2023a. VEB.RF is a state corporation established by Russian federal law as a national economic development institution (VEB.RF, "Investment for Development," homepage, undated).

[170] As of September 2023, public domestic debt of the Russian Federation was $20.3 trillion rubles, less than 15 percent of its nominal 2022 GDP (for debt statistics, see Ministry of Finance of the Russian Federation, "Public Domestic Debt of the Russian Federation," September 13, 2023b).

Abbreviations

AFV	armored fighting vehicle
ALCM	air-launched cruise missile
APC	armored personnel carrier
ASCM	anti-ship cruise missile
BTG	battalion tactical group
COVID-19	coronavirus disease 2019
ESPO	East Siberia-Pacific Ocean pipeline system
EU	European Union
GDP	gross domestic product
IFV	infantry fighting vehicle
KIA	killed in action
MBT	main battle tank
MRL	multiple rocket launcher
SLCM	sea-launched cruise missile
SPA	self-propelled artillery
SRBM	short-range ballistic missile
UAV	unmanned aerial vehicle

Bibliography

"Anti-War Wave [АНТИВОЕННАЯ ВОЛНА]," OK Russians, webpage, 2022. As of August 30, 2022:
https://research-march.okrussians.org/

Axe, David, "In 100 Days, a Separatist Army in Ukraine Lost Half Its Troops," *Forbes*, June 13, 2022a.

Axe, David, "The Russian Army Has Lost More Than 300 Artillery Pieces in Ukraine. Old Howitzers Could Replace Them," *Forbes*, July 27, 2022b.

Bank of Russia, "The Bank of Russia Increases the Key Rate by 100 b.p. to 9.50% p.a.," press release, February 11, 2022a.

Bank of Russia, "Bank of Russia's Medium-Term Forecast Following the Bank of Russia Board of Directors' Key Rate Meeting on 11 February 2022," press release, February 11, 2022b.

Bank of Russia, "Bank of Russia Increases the Key Rate to 20% p.a.," press release, February 28, 2022c.

Bank of Russia, *Regional Economy: Commentaries by Bank of Russia Main Branches*, No. 11, April 2022d.

Bank of Russia, "The Bank of Russia Cuts the Key Rate by 300 b.p. to 17.00% p.a.," press release, April 8, 2022e.

Bank of Russia, "Elvira Nabiullina's Speech at Joint Meeting of State Duma Dedicated Committees on Bank of Russia's 2021 Annual Report," April 18, 2022f.

Bank of Russia, "The Bank of Russia Cuts the Key Rate by 300 b.p. to 14.00% p.a.," press release, April 29, 2022g.

Bank of Russia, "Statement by Bank of Russia Governor Elvira Nabiullina in Follow-Up to Board of Directors Meeting on 29 April 2022," April 29, 2022h.

Bank of Russia, "Bank of Russia Cuts Key Rate by 300 bp to 11.00% p.a.," press release, May 26, 2022i.

Bank of Russia, "Bank of Russia Cuts Key Rate by 150 bp to 9.50% p.a.," press release, June 10, 2022j.

Bank of Russia, *Regional Economy: Commentaries by Bank of Russia Main Branches*, No. 13, July 2022k.

Bank of Russia, "Balance of Payments of the Russian Federation (in US$ Million), Standard Components [Платежный баланс Российской Федерации (в млн долларов США) Стандартные компоненты]," Excel spreadsheet, July 7, 2022l. As of August 29, 2022: http://www.cbr.ru/statistics/macro_itm/svs/p_balance/

Bank of Russia, "Bank of Russia Cuts Key Rate by 150 b.p. to 8.00% p.a.," press release, July 22, 2022m.

Bank of Russia "Bank of Russia's Medium-Term Forecast Following the Bank of Russia Board of Directors' Key Rate Meeting on 22 July 2022," press release, July 22, 2022n.

Bank of Russia, "Statement by Bank of Russia Governor Elvira Nabiullina in Follow-Up to Board of Directors Meeting on 22 July 2022," press release, July 22, 2022o.

Bank of Russia, *Balance of Payments, Russian Federation* [Платежный Баланс, Российской Федерации], Vol. 11, Nos. 1–2, July 26, 2022p.

Bank of Russia, "Bank of Russia Cuts Key Rate by 50 b.p. to 7.50% p.a.," press release, September 16, 2022q.

Bank of Russia, International Reserves of the Russian Federation (End of Period), online data, last updated September 16, 2022r. As of September 24, 2022: https://www.cbr.ru/eng/hd_base/mrrf/mrrf_7d/

Bank of Russia, *October 2022 Monetary Policy Report*, No. 4, November 8, 2022s.

Bank of Russia, *Monetary Policy Report, February 2023*, No. 1, February 20, 2023a.

Bank of Russia, "Bank of Russia Increases Key Rate by 100 b.p. to 8.50% p.a.," press release, July 21, 2023b.

Bank of Russia, "Statement by Bank of Russia Governor Elvira Nabiullina in Follow-Up to Board of Directors Meeting on 21 July 2023," speech, July 21, 2023c.

Bank of Russia, *Russia's Balance of Payments, Information and Analytical Commentary*, No. 2, Vol. 15, July 25, 2023d.

Bank of Russia, "Bank of Russia Increases Key Rate by 350 b.p. to 12.50% p.a.," press release, August 15, 2023e.

Bank of Russia, *Regional Economy: Commentaries by Bank of Russia Main Branches*, No. 22, September 6, 2023f.

Bank of Russia, "Bank of Russia Increases Key Rate by 100 b.p. to 13.00% p.a.," press release, Press Service of the Bank of Russia, September 15, 2023g.

Bank of Russia "Bank of Russia's Medium-Term Forecast Following the Bank of Russia Board of Directors' Key Rate Meeting on 15 September 2023," press release, September 15, 2023h.

Bank of Russia, "Statement by Bank of Russia Governor Elvira Nabiullina in Follow-Up to Board of Directors Meeting on 15 September 2023," press release, September 15, 2023i.

Bank of Russia, "Bank of Russia Extends Restrictions for Non-Residents from Unfriendly Countries to Transfer Money Abroad from Brokerage and Trust Management Accounts," press release, September 26, 2023j.

Bank of Russia, "Bank of Russia Extends Restrictions on Money Transfers Abroad for Another Six Months," press release, September 29, 2023k.

Barnes, Julian E., Eric Schmitt, and Thomas Gibbons-Neff, "Russia Overcomes Sanctions to Expand Missile Production, Officials Say," *New York Times*, September 13, 2023.

Beardsworth, James, "Uptick in Combat Missions Signals Changing Role for Russia's Air Force in Ukraine," *Moscow Times*, May 11, 2022.

Belasco, Amy, *The Cost of Iraq, Afghanistan, and Other Global War on Terror Operations Since 9/11*, Congressional Research Service, RL33110, December 8, 2014.

"The Belorussian Military Is Selling Two An-26 Aircraft [Белорусские военные продают два самолета Ан-26]," *RIA Novosti*, February 13, 2014.

Berman, Gavin, "The Cost of International Military Operations," Standard Note SN/SG/3139, United Kingdom House of Commons, July 5, 2012.

"Big Differences Across Sectoral Contractions in Russia," BOFIT Weekly 2022/31, The Bank of Finland Institute for Emerging Economies, August 5, 2022.

Borger, Julian, "Russia Deploys Up to 20,000 Mercenaries in Battle for Ukraine's Donbas Region," *The Guardian*, April 19, 2022.

Bort, Christopher, "Why the Kremlin Lies: Understanding Its Loose Relationship with the Truth," Carnegie Endowment for International Peace, January 6, 2022.

Boussel, Pierre, "Syrian Mercenaries in Ukraine: Delusion or Reality," *Sada*, Carnegie Endowment for International Peace, June 23, 2022.

Brimelow, Benjamin, "Russia Is Using Its Newest and Oldest Missiles Indiscriminately Against Ukraine," *Business Insider*, July 31, 2022.

Brooks, Robin [@RobinBrooksIIF], "The insurance needed to operate these oil tankers is provided mainly out of the UK," Twitter post, August 24, 2022a. As of August 26, 2022: https://twitter.com/RobinBrooksIIF/status/1562421368745914369

Brooks, Robin [@RobinBrooksIIF], "We got many questions on this chart, which shows Greek oil tankers carrying the bulk of Russian oil," Twitter post, August 24, 2022b. As of August 26, 2022: https://twitter.com/RobinBrooksIIF/status/1562418194882740225

Bryson, John, "Russia as a Low-Tech Nation—Severing the Country from Global Supply Chains with the Ukrainian War," University of Birmingham, June 17, 2022.

Bychkovska, Yulia, Ana Mikadze, and Jacob Saionz, *Working Hard or Hardly Working? Understanding the Sanctions' Effects on Russia's Economy and War Effort*, Maxwell School at Syracuse University, June 20, 2023. As of November 9, 2023:
https://drive.google.com/file/d/1QWmVPalN8j2M9ikEdtW22ybks4BiWUW0/view?pli=1

Cappella, Rosella, *The Political Economy of War Finance*, dissertation, University of Pennsylvania, 2012.

Center for Strategic and International Studies Missile Defense Project [@Missile_Defense], "Russian Missile Attacks on Ukraine," Twitter account, June 29, 2022.

Chief Executive Leadership Institute, "Over 1,000 Companies Have Curtailed Operations in Russia—But Some Remain," updated by Jeffrey Sonnenfeld and Yale Research Team: Meena Ambati, Wiktor Babinski, Will Berkley, Ahaan Bhansali, Yash Bhansali, Forrest Michael Bomann, Michal Boron, Tristan Brigham, Jesse Bross, Adnan Bseisu, Katie Burke, Lauren Cho, Cara Chong, Andrea Chwedczuk, Adriana Coleska, Maia Cook, Cam Coyle, Khulan Erdenedalai, Paola Flores Sanchez, Jake Seymour Garza, Kevin Grold, Tamara Gruslova, Hunter Harmon, Patrik Haverinen, Georgia Hirsty, Warner Hoshide, Daniel Jensen, Aditya Kabra, Nolan Kaputa, Mateusz Kasprowicz, Jay Kauffin, Sahana Kaur, Yuto Kida, Ava Leipzig, Victoria Liando, Cate Littlefield, Kasey Maguire, Marek Malinowski, Maksimas Milta, Rémi Moët-Buonaparte, Atin Narain, Christophe Navarre, Marina Negroponte, Camillo Padulli, Jeremy Perkins, Katya Pinchuk, Yevheniia Podurets, Aranyo Ray, Dorothea Robertson, Eleanor Schoenbrun, Nick Shcherban, Franek Sokolowski, Andrew Sonneborn, David Sun, Christopher Sylvester, Steven Tian, Maria Trybus, Umid Usmanov, Ryan Vakil, Daria Valska, Bryson Wiese, Chris Wright, Michal Wyrebkowski, Nicole Xing, Lara Yellin, Steven Zaslavsky, Nick Zeffiro, and Grace Zhang, Yale School of Management, Yale University, last updated August 30, 2022.

"Crisis in Russian Economy Developing Along Flatter Trajectory, Signs of Stabilization Already Apparent—Central Bank," Interfax-Ukraine, July 12, 2022.

"Concise Information on the Execution of the Federal Budget [Краткая информация об исполнении федерального бюджета]," Russian Ministry of Finance, Spring 2022.

"Contract Service [Служба по контракту]," Soyuz Prizyvnikov Rossii, August 31, 2022.

"Contractees in BTGs," *Russian Defense Policy*, blog post, September 17, 2016. As of August 29, 2022:
https://russiandefpolicy.com/2016/09/17/contractees-in-btgs/

Cooper, Helene, "Heavy Losses Leave Russia Short of Its Goal, U.S. Officials Say," *New York Times*, August 11, 2022.

Cooper, Julian, *Russian Military Expenditure: Data, Analysis and Issues*, FOI-R—3688—SE, FOI, Swedish Defense Research Agency, September 2013.

Cooper, Julian, *Russia's Military Expenditure During Its War Against Ukraine*, Stockholm International Peace Research Institute, June 2023.

Copp, Tara, "Russian Jets Flying 200 Sorties a Day, but Firing from Their Own Airspace, Pentagon Says," *Defense One*, March 11, 2022.

"The Cost of the BTR-82A and Its Capabilities [Стоимость БТР-82А и его возможности]," Zen.yandex, blog post, October 11, 2018.

Delegation of the European Union to the Holy See, Order of Malta, United Nations Organisations in Rome and to the Republic of San Marino, "EU Sanctions Do Not Restrict EU and Third Countries' Trade in Agrifood Products," press release, June 24, 2022.

Department of Employment of the Amur Region [Управление занятости населения Амурской области / Upravlenie zaniatosti naseleniia Amurskoi oblasti], Vkontakte, webpage, November 16, 2022. As of October 5, 2023:
https://vk.com/wall-211340212_293

Department of the Army, *Department of Defense Fiscal Year (FY) 2020 Budget Estimates, Procurement of Weapons and Tracked Combat Vehicles, Army*, March 2019.

Dezan Shira & Associates, "Moscow Stock Exchange Resumes Selected Trading," *Russia Briefing*, March 21, 2022.

Druyan Feldman, Bat Chen, and Arkady Mil-Man, "The War in Ukraine: Exacerbating Russia's Demographic Crisis," Institute for National Security Studies, August 22, 2023.

Dyner, Anna Maria, *Assessment of the Russian Armed Forces' State Armament Programme in 2011–2020*, Polish Institute of International Affairs, June 2021.

"Exclusive: Russia Starts Stripping Jetliners for Parts as Sanctions Bite," Reuters, August 9, 2022.

European Commission, "Russia's War on Ukraine: EU Adopts Sixth Package of Sanctions Against Russia," press release, June 3, 2022.

European Council and Council of the European Union, "Timeline—EU Restrictive Measures Against Russia over Ukraine," webpage, last reviewed on September 14, 2022. As of September 24, 2022:
https://www.consilium.europa.eu/en/policies/sanctions/restrictive-measures-against-russia-over-ukraine/history-restrictive-measures-against-russia-over-ukraine/

"Exchange Rates United Kingdom," webpage, 2022. As of December 27, 2022:
https://www.exchangerates.org.uk/

Fabrichnaya, Elena, and Alexander Marrow, "Russia to Spend $6.8 Billion From Wealth Fund on Infrastructure Projects in 2022," Reuters, September 23, 2022.

Federal State Statistical Service (Rosstat), "Second GDP Estimate 2021 [Вторая оценка ВВП за 2021 год]," Moscow, April 8, 2022a.

Federal State Statistical Service (Rosstat), "Rosstat Presents the First Estimate of GDP for the 1st Quarter [Росстат представляет первую оценку ВВП за I квартал 2022года]," Moscow, June 17, 2022b.

Federal State Statistical Service (Rosstat), "GDP Quarters (Since 1995), Gross Domestic Product, National Accounts, Statistics," Excel spreadsheet, August 12, 2022c. As of August 24, 2022:
https://rosstat.gov.ru/storage/mediabank/VVP_kvartal_s%201995.xls

Federal State Statistical Service (Rosstat), "On a Preliminary Estimate of GDP Dynamics in the II Quarter of 2022 [О предварительной оценке динамики ВВП во II квартале 2022 года]," Moscow, August 12, 2022d.

Federal State Statistical Service (Rosstat), "About Industrial Production in January–July 2022 [О промышленном производстве в январе-июле 2022 года]," August 24, 2022e.

Federal State Statistical Service (Rosstat), "On the Production and Use of Gross Domestic Product (GDP) in 2022 [О производстве и использовании валового внутреннего продукта (ВВП) в 2022 году]," April 7, 2023a.

Federal State Statistical Service (Rosstat), "On Production of Gross Domestic Product in the First Quarter of 2023 [О Производстве Валового Внутреннего Продукта В I Квартале 2023 Года]," June 15, 2023b.

Federal State Statistical Service (Rosstat), "GDP Years (Since 1995) [ВВП годы (с 1995 г.)]," spreadsheet, July 4, 2023c.

Federal State Statistical Service (Rosstat), "GDP Quarters (Since 1995) [ВВП кварталы (с 1995 г.)]," spreadsheet, August 9, 2023d.

Federal State Statistical Service (Rosstat), "On Production of Gross Domestic Product in the Second Quarter of 2023 [О Производстве Валового Внутреннего Продукта В Ii Квартале 2023 Года]," September 8, 2023e.

Federal State Statistical Service (Rosstat), "About Industrial Production in January–August 2023 [О промышленном производстве в январе–Август 2023 года]," September 27, 2023f.

Filatiev, Pavel, *ZOV*, Vkontakte, August 1, 2022.

"The FSB is Buying Five Mi-35M Helicopters [ФСБ России закупит пять вертолетов Ми-35M]," Centre for Analysis of Strategy and Technologies, blog post, July 9, 2015.

Gauthier-Villars, David, Steve Stecklow, Maurice Tamman, Stephen Grey, and Andrew Macaskill, "As Russian Missiles Struck Ukraine, Western Tech Still Flowed," *Reuters*, August 8, 2022.

Geist, Edward, "Appendix F: Indirect Fires," in Andrew Radin, Lynn E. Davis, Edward Geist, Eugeniu Han, Dara Massicot, Matthew Povlock, Clint Reach, Scott Boston, Samuel Charap, William Mackenzie, Katya Migacheva, Trevor Johnston, and Austin Long, *The Future of the Russian Military: Russia's Ground Combat Capabilities and Implications for U.S.-Russia Competition*, RAND Corporation, RR-3099-A, 2018. As of May 3, 2023: https://www.rand.org/pubs/research_reports/RR3099.html

GoldPrice, homepage, 2022. As of December 27, 2022: https://goldprice.org/

Grachev, V. V., "Analysis of the Problems of Material Support of the Battalion Tactical Group Revealed During a Special Exercise with Military Governance Bodies, Brigades, Military Units and Logistics Organizations of the Central Military District," *Herald of the Volsk Military Institute of Logistics*, Vol. 2, No. 38, 2016.

Grau, Lester W., and Charles K. Bartles, *The Russian Way of War: Force Structure, Tactics, and Modernization of the Russian Ground Forces*, Foreign Military Studies Office, 2016.

Griffin, Rosemary, Elza Turner, Nick Coleman, and Alexander Bor, "Ukraine War Sees Diesel Prices Rise as Russia's Thirsty Battle Tanks Guzzle Fuel," S&P Global Commodity Insights, May 23, 2022.

Hobson, Peter, "Calculating the Cost of Russia's War in Syria," *Moscow Times*, October 20, 2015.

"How Much Russian Military Armor Costs [Сколько стоит бронетехника Российской армии]," Ferra.ru, March 4, 2022.

"'If You Didn't Follow Instructions, They Shot You': A Russian Convict Recruited by the Wagner Group Tells His Story," *Meduza.io*, September 16, 2022.

"In Russia, Ammunition Stocks Were Created for 70 Years: A Military Expert Told How Much They Would be Enough," *West Observer*, July 26, 2022.

Interfax-Ukraine, "Kyiv Says There Are About 6,000 Russian Soldiers, 40,000 Separatists in Donbas," *Kyiv Post*, September 11, 2017.

International Energy Agency, World Energy Outlook 2022, Paris, "Russian Oil Exports in the World Energy Outlook, 2022 vs. 2021," webpage, last updated October 26, 2022. As of December 27, 2022: https://www.iea.org/data-and-statistics/charts/russian-oil-exports-in-the-world-energy-outlook-2022-vs-2021

International Energy Agency, World Energy Outlook 2022, Paris, "Russian Gas Exports in the World Energy Outlook, 2022 vs. 2021," webpage, last updated November 3, 2022. As of December 27, 2022:
https://www.iea.org/data-and-statistics/charts/russian-gas-exports-in-the-world-energy-outlook-2022-vs-2021

International Institute for Strategic Studies, *The Military Balance 2020*, 1st ed., Routledge, 2020.

International Monetary Fund, *World Economic Outlook Update: Rising Caseloads, A Disrupted Recovery, and Higher Inflation*, January 2022a.

International Monetary Fund, *World Economic Outlook Update: War Sets Back the Global Recovery*, April 2022b.

International Monetary Fund, *World Economic Outlook Update: Gloomy and More Uncertain*, July 2022c.

International Monetary Fund, *World Economic Outlook Update: Near-Term Resilience, Persistent Challenges*, July 2023.

Janovksy, Jakub, naalsio26, Aloha, Dan, and Kemal, "Attack on Europe: Documenting Russian Equipment Losses During the Russian Invasion of Ukraine," Oryx, February 24, 2022. Last updated October 5, 2023:
https://www.oryxspioenkop.com/2022/02/attack-on-europe-documenting-equipment.html

Kaonga, Gerrard, "Russia Failing to Properly Pay, Feed Military Recruits in Ukraine—Report," *Newsweek*, August 15, 2022.

Karam, Zeina, "Explainer: Will Russia Bring Syrian Fighters to Ukraine?" Associated Press, March 11, 2022.

Khurshudyan, Isabelle, and Paul Sonne, "Russia Targeted Ukrainian Ammunition to Weaken Kyiv on the Battlefield," *Washington Post*, June 24, 2022.

Kofman, Michael, and Rob Lee, "Not Built for Purpose: The Russian Military's Ill-Fated Force Design," *War on the Rocks*, June 2, 2022.

Korsunskaya, Darya, and Alexander Marrow, "'Everything for the Front': Russia Allots a Third of 2024 Spending to Defence," Reuters, October 2, 2023.

Lau, Yvonne, "'We Realized That There's No Way We Can Return': Russia's Best and Brightest Are Leaving the Country in Record Numbers. 6 Young Russians Explain Why They Left," *Fortune*, August 20, 2022.

Lavrov, Anton, and Bogdan Stepovoi, "'Superalligator' for a Billion Rubles: The Ministry of Defense Confirmed the Price of New Helicopters [«Суператлигатор» за миллиард: Минобороны утвердило цену новых вертолетов]," *Izvestiya*, October 4, 2021.

Lee, Rob [@RALee85], "This looks like a Kh-31P air-launched anti-radar missile wreckage reportedly in Kyiv," Twitter post, February 23, 2022. As of March 22, 2023:
https://twitter.com/RALee85/status/1496734690971197444

Liakhov, Peter [@peterliakhov], "A snapshot of the Russian economy," Twitter post, March 3, 2022. As of August 19, 2022:
https://twitter.com/peterliakhov/status/1499341576518217730

Lichfield, Charles, *Windfall: How Russia Managed Oil and Gas Income After Invading Ukraine, and How it Will Have to Make Do with Less*, Atlantic Council, November 30, 2022.

Lisitsyna, Maria, "Putin Revealed Compensation Figures to Injured and Families of Fallen Soldiers in Ukraine [Путин раскрыл выплаты раненым и семьям погибших на Украине военных]," RBC, March 3, 2022.

Litovkin, Dmitrii, "The T-72 Tanks Got the 'Relikt' [Танкам Т-72 прописали «Реликт»]," *Izvestiya*, March 10, 2016.

Martin, Richard, "Sanctions Against Russia—A Timeline," S&P Global, webpage, December 21, 2022. As of December 27, 2022:
https://www.spglobal.com/marketintelligence/en/news-insights/latest-news-headlines/sanctions-against-russia-8211-a-timeline-69602559

Maskin, V. M., "On the Issue of Maintaining Constant Readiness Formations and Combat Units [К вопросу о содержании соединенийеи воинских частей в категории постоянной готовности]," *Military Thought*, No. 1, 2010

McCulla, Stephanie H., and Shelly Smith, *Measuring the Economy: A Primer on GDP and the National Income and Product Accounts*, Bureau of Economic Analysis, U.S. Department of Commerce, December 2015.

Milanovic, Branko, "Russia's Long-Term Economic Prospects," *Global Inequality and More 3.0*, March 11, 2022a.

Milanovic, Branko, "The Novelty of Technologically Regressive Import Substitution," *Global Policy*, May 18, 2022b.

Ministry of Defense, presentation, 2012–2020. As of September 26, 2022:
http://mil.ru/files/files/2012-2020.pdf

"The Ministry of Defense Will Buy 140 Ka-52 Helicopters [Минобороны купит более 140 вертолётов Ka-52]," RBC, September 3, 2011.

Ministry of Finance of the Russian Federation, Federal Budget, spreadsheet, undated.

Ministry of Finance of the Russian Federation, Federal Budget, spreadsheet, February 11, 2022a.

Ministry of Finance of the Russian Federation, "Volume of the National Wealth Fund," February 24, 2022b.

Ministry of Finance of the Russian Federation, "Allocation of the National Wealth Fund's Assets to Deposits in VEB.RF," webpage, September 9, 2023a. As of October 6, 2023:
https://minfin.gov.ru/en/document?id_4=114232-
allocation_of_national_wealth_funds_assets_to_deposits_in_veb.rf

Ministry of Finance of the Russian Federation, "Public Domestic Debt of the Russian Federation," webpage, last updated October 10, 2023b. As of November 8, 2023:
https://minfin.gov.ru/en/policy_issues/debt/domestic/structure?id_4=104307-
public_domestic_debt_of_the_russian_federtation

Ministry of Finance of the Russian Federation, "Volume of the National Wealth Fund," webpage, October 17, 2023c. As of November 8, 2023:
https://minfin.gov.ru/en/document?id_4=104686-volume_of_the_national_wealth_fund

Ministry of Finance of the Russian Federation, "Federal Budget," spreadsheet, September 21, 2023d.

Mitzer, Stijn, and Jakub Janovsky, in collaboration with Joost Oliemans, Kemal, Dan, and naalsio26, "Attack on Europe: Documenting Russian Equipment Losses During the 2022 Russian Invasion of Ukraine," Oryx, August 2, 2022.

"Mobilization and the SMO (Special Military Operation). The Key Points of Sergei Shoigu's Speech [Мобилизация и СВО. Главные тезисы выступления Сергея Шойгу]," Smotrim.ru, September 21, 2022.

Morpurgo, Giulia, and Libby Cherry, "Russia Slips into Historic Default as Sanctions Muddy Next Steps," Bloomberg, June 26, 2022.

Moscow Exchange, "Moscow Exchange Announces Results for the Full Year 2020," press release, March 5, 2021a.

Moscow Exchange, "Moscow Exchange Announces Results for the First Quarter of 2021," press release, April 30, 2021b.

Moscow Exchange, "Moscow Exchange Announces Results for the Second Quarter of 2021," press release, August 20, 2021c.

Moscow Exchange, "Moscow Exchange Announces Results for the Third Quarter of 2021," press release, October 29, 2021d.

Moscow Exchange, "Moscow Exchange Has Suspended Trading on All of its Markets Until Further Notice," press release, February 24, 2022a.

Moscow Exchange, "Moscow Exchange Resumes Trading on its Markets at 10:00am," press release, February 24, 2022b.

Moscow Exchange, "Moscow Exchange Announces Results for the Full Year 2021," press release, March 4, 2022c.

Moscow Exchange, "Moscow Exchange Announces Results for Q1 2022," press release, April 29, 2022d.

Moscow Exchange, "Moscow Exchange Announces Results for Q2 2022," press release, August 19, 2022e.

Moscow Exchange, "Moscow Exchange Announces Results for Q3 2022," press release, November 3, 2022f.

Moscow Exchange, "RUABITR Bond Index," webpage, 2022g. As of December 30, 2022: https://www.moex.com/en/index/RUABITR/

Moscow Exchange, "Moscow Exchange Announces Results for the Full Year 2022," press release, March 10, 2023a.

Moscow Exchange, "Moscow Exchange Announces Results for the First Quarter of 2023," press release, May 22, 2023b.

Moscow Exchange, "Moscow Exchange Announces Results for the second Quarter of 2023," press release, August 23, 2023c.

"Moscow Exchange to Resume Shares and Bond Trading in Normal Mode on Monday," Reuters, March 26, 2022.

"MSTA-SV," Deagel.com, August 31, 2022.

"MT-LB, Artillery Hauler. Its Cost [МТ-ЛБ" артиллерийский тягач. Его стоимость]," Zen.yandex, blog post, October 30, 2018.

"Much of Russia's Intellectual Elite Has Fled the Country," *The Economist*, August 9, 2022.

Mueller, Karl, ed., *Precision and Purpose: Air Power in the Libyan Civil War*, RAND Corporation, RR-676-AF, 2011. As of May 3, 2023: https://www.rand.org/pubs/research_reports/RR676.html

"Nearly 4M Russians Left Russia in Early 2022—FSB," *Moscow Times*, May 6, 2022.

"New Su-25: The Cost of the 'Supergracha' Has Been Revealed [Новый Су-25: стала известна стоимость «Суперграча»]," Warfiles.ru, August 31, 2022.

Organization for Economic Co-operation and Development, National Currency to US Dollar Exchange Rate: Average of Daily Rates for the Russian Federation [CCUSMA02RUM618N], retrieved from FRED, Federal Reserve Bank of St. Louis, August 2, 2022. As of August 2, 2022:
https://fred.stlouisfed.org/series/CCUSMA02RUM618N

Parfonov, Hlib, "Ukrainian Strikes Cause Moscow to Re-Think Munitions Supply and Logistics (Part Two)," *Eurasia Daily Monitor*, Vol. 19, No. 127, August 18, 2022.

Peltier, Heidi, *The Growth of the 'Camo Economy' and the Commercialization of the Post-9/11 Wars*, Watson Institute at Brown University and Pardee Center at Boston University, June 30, 2020.

Perkins, Robert, "Russia's Seaborne Oil Exports Rise in August as Sanctions Impact Remains Muted," S&P Global Commodity Insights, August 18, 2022.

President of Russia, Decree on the Announcement of Partial Mobilization in the Russian Federation [Указ «Об объявлении частичной мобилизации в Российской Федерации]," Decree No. 647, September 21, 2022.

"Putin Orders Measures to Reverse Mass Wartime Exodus," *Moscow Times*, May 12, 2023.

Re: Russia, "Escape from War: New Data Puts the Number of Russians Who Have Left at More than 800,000," *Review*, July 2023.

Roblin, Sebastien, "Russia Is Upgrading Its Supersonic Su-34 'Hellduck' Bombers," *National Interest*, May 15, 2021.

Rusia en España [@EmbajadaRusaES], "Time to move to Russia," Twitter post, July 29, 2022. As of August 30, 2022:
https://twitter.com/EmbajadaRusaES/status/1552886338926479360

"Russia Ramping Up Ukraine Strikes with Less Precise Soviet-Era Missiles—General," Reuters, June 30, 2022.

"Russia Suspends Publication of Import-Export Data to Avoid 'Speculation'" Reuters, April 21, 2022.

"Russian Economy Ministry Expects Inflation to Reach 13.4% in 2022, GDP to Drop to 4.2%," TASS, August 16, 2022.

"Russian GDP Growth Slows to 1.6% in March, Estimated at 3.7% in Q1—Econ Ministry," Interfax-Ukraine, April 28, 2022.

"Russians Have Emigrated in Huge Numbers Since the War in Ukraine," *The Economist*, August 23, 2023.

"Russia's Federal Budget Sees Exceptional Drop in Revenues in July; Spending Continues to Rise," BOFIT Weekly 2022/33, The Bank of Finland Institute for Emerging Economies, August 19, 2022.

"Sanctions Have Frozen Around $300 Bln of Russian Reserves, FinMin Says," Reuters, March 13, 2022.

Savelov, Alexei, "The Number of Military Servicemembers on Contract in the Russian Military Has More Than Doubled [Численность военнослужащих по контракту в российской армии возросла более чем в два раза]," *Tvzvezda*, June 11, 2018.

Shelbourne, Mallory, "Raytheon Awarded $217M Tomahawk Missiles Contract for Navy, Marines, Army," *USNI News*, May 25, 2022

Schwirtz, Michael, Marc Santora, and Matthew Mpoke Bigg, "Ukraine Pushes to Retake Ground in the South as Russia Pours in Reinforcements," *New York Times*, July 28, 2022.

Shemelov, Stanislav, and Maksim Kirilov, "The Word 'Battalion' Is Too Much: How the Named Units Are Standing in for Mobilization in Russia [Слово «батальон» здесь чересчур преувеличено»: как именные подразделения заменяют в России мобилизацию]," *BiznesOnline*, August 24, 2022.

Siderkova, Inna, "The Ministry of Defense Will Receive 24 'Flying Tanks' to Test in Syria [Минобороны получит 24 «летающих танка» для испытания в Сирии]," RBC, October 19, 2017.

Solopov, Maksim, and Aleksandr Artem'ev, "RBC Investigation: How Much is Russia Spending on its War in Syria [Расследование РБК: сколько тратит Россия на войну в Сирии]," RBC, October 28, 2015.

Sonnenfeld, Jeffrey A., Steven Tian, Franek Sokolowski, Michal Wyrebkowski, Mateusz Kasprowicz, and Yale Chief Executive Leadership Institute Researchers, *Business Retreats and Sanctions are Crippling the Russian Economy: Measures of Current Economic Activity and Economic Outlook Point to Devastating Impact on Russia*, Yale University, July 2022.

Starostina, Yulia, "Secret Economy: What Hiding the Stats Does for Russia," Carnegie Endowment for International Peace, July 1, 2022.

Statista Research Department, "Average Monthly Price of Urals Crude Oil from January 2018 to July 2022 (in U.S. Dollars per Barrel)," database, August 11, 2022a. As of August 26, 2022: https://www.statista.com/statistics/1112243/urals-crude-oil-price/

Statista Research Department, "Number of Active Business Enterprises in Russia from 2017 to 2021 (in Millions)," database, October 10, 2022b. As of December 27, 2022: https://www.statista.com/statistics/1337527/business-enterprises-russia/

Statista Research Department, "Average Monthly Price of Urals Crude Oil from January 2007 to August 2023," dataset, September 13, 2023. As of October 3, 2023: https://www.statista.com/statistics/1112243/urals-crude-oil-price/

Suvorov, Sergei, "The Ural 'Proryv': Why the New Russian T-90M is Worth Two Abrams [Уральский «Прорыв»: Почему новый российский танк т-90M стоит двух «Абрамсов»]," TVzvezda, February 2, 2018.

Tkachev, Ivan, and Iuliia Vyrodova, "The Ministry of Finance in Connection with the Sanctions Classified Budget Expenditures in Areas [Минфин в связи с санкциями засекретил расходы бюджета по направлениям]," RBC, June 14, 2022.

"Tornado-G MRL to Complete State Trials," *Janes*, undated.

"The Troops of the Russian Federation Near Ukraine Number About 149,000 People and May Increase by Several Thousand More in the Coming Days [Війська РФ поблизу України налічують близько 149 тис. осіб і найближчими днями можуть зрости ще на кілька тисяч]," Interfax-Ukraine, February 18, 2022.

Trinko, Myroslav, "Ukrainian Air Defense Forces Shot Down Two Kalibr Cruise Missiles Worth Almost $2,000,000 Fired from A Russian Submarine in the Black Sea," Gagadget.com, July 6, 2022.

Tsvetkova, Maria, "Some Wounded Russian Soldiers Find Compensation Elusive, Despite Putin's Pledge," Reuters, July 29, 2022.

Tuchkov, Vladimir, "Whose UAVs Are the Best: Israeli, American, or Russian? [Чьи беспилотники лучше: израильские, американские или российские?]," *Svobodnaya Pressa*, November 2, 2014.

Tversky, Amos, and Daniel Kahneman, "Judgment Under Uncertainty: Heuristics and Biases," *Science*, New Series, Vol. 185, No. 4157, September 27, 1974.

United Kingdom Foreign Commonwealth and Development Office, "UK Sanctions Following Russia's Invasion of Ukraine," webpage, last updated July 26, 2022. As of September 24, 2022: https://www.gov.uk/government/collections/uk-sanctions-following-russias-invasion-of-ukraine

United States Census Bureau, International Database, online database, last revised December 21, 2021. As of August 30, 2022: https://www.census.gov/programs-surveys/international-programs/about/idb.html

U.S. Department of Commerce, "Commerce Implements Sweeping Restrictions on Exports to Russia in Response to Further Invasion of Ukraine," press release, February 24, 2022.

U.S. Department of Defense, "Fact Sheet on U.S. Security Assistance to Ukraine," fact sheet, November 4, 2022.

U.S. Department of the Treasury, "U.S. Treasury Announces Unprecedented and Expansive Sanctions Against Russia, Imposing Swift and Severe Economic Costs," press release, February 24, 2022a.

U.S. Department of the Treasury, "U.S. Treasury Imposes Sanctions on Russian Federation President Vladimir Putin and Minister of Foreign Affairs Sergei Lavrov," press release, February 25, 2022b.

U.S. Department of the Treasury, "Treasury Prohibits Transactions with Central Bank of Russia and Imposes Sanctions on Key Sources of Russia's Wealth," press release, February 28, 2022c.

U.S. Department of the Treasury, "Treasury Sanctions Russians Bankrolling Putin and Russia-Backed Influence Actors," press release, March 3, 2022d.

U.S. Department of the Treasury, "Treasury Sanctions Kremlin Elites, Leaders, Oligarchs, and Family for Enabling Putin's War Against Ukraine," press release, March 11, 2022e.

U.S. Department of the Treasury, "Treasury Releases Fact Sheet on Food and Fertilizer-Related Authorizations Under Russia Sanctions; Expands General License Authorizing Agricultural Transactions," press release, July 14, 2022f.

U.S. Energy Information Administration, "Europe Brent Spot Price FOB (Dollars per Barrel)," dataset, August 24, 2022, and December 29, 2022. As of December 30, 2022: https://www.eia.gov/dnav/pet/hist/RBRTED.htm

U.S. Energy Information Administration, "Europe Brent Spot Price FOB (Dollars per Barrel)," dataset, September 27, 2023. As of November 8, 2023: https://www.eia.gov/dnav/pet/hist/RBRTED.htm

U.S. International Trade Commission, Dataweb, online database, 2022. As of August 31, 2022: https://dataweb.usitc.gov/

U.S. Senate, Committee on Armed Services, "Summary of the Fiscal Year 2022 National Defense Authorization Act," December 7, 2021.

VEB.RF, "Investment for Development," homepage, undated. As of November 8, 2023: https://xn--90ab5f.xn--p1ai/en/

Verma, Mimansa, "Days After Cautioning Putin on War, India May Skip Russian ESPO-Crude Oil Import," Quartz India, September 23, 2022.

Verma, Nidhi, "India Set to Skip Buying Russia's ESPO Crude in Sept as Freight Costs Jump," Reuters, September 22. 2022.

Vikulov, S. F. (ed.), *Contemporary Issues in the Realization of the Military-Economic Potential of Russia in the First Quarter of the 21st Century and the Primary Areas for Military-Economic Research* [Актуальные проблемы реализации военно-экономического потенциала России в первой четверти XXI века и основные направления военно-экономических исследований], Book 2, Kantsler, 2019.

Vinokurov, Andrei, "Special Volunteer Operation [Специальная добровольческая операция]," *Kommersant*, August 8, 2022.

Watling, Jack, and Nick Reynolds, *Special Report: Ukraine at War: Paving the Road from Survival to Victory*, Royal United Services Institute for Defence and Security Studies, July 4, 2022.

Westerlund, Fredrik, Susanne Oxenstierna, Gudrun Persson, Jonas Kjellén, Johan Norberg, Jakob Hedenskog, Tomas Malmlöf, Martin Goliath, Johan Engvall, and Nils Dahlqvist, *Russian Military Capability in a Ten-Year Perspective 2019*, FOI, FOI-R-4758, 2019.

"What Is Russia's Wagner Group of Mercenaries in Ukraine?" BBC, August 16, 2022.

World Bank, *Global Economic Prospects*, January 2022a.

World Bank, World Development Indicators, online database, last updated July 20, 2022b. As of August 24, 2022:
https://databank.worldbank.org/source/world-development-indicators

Zverev, Anton, "Moscow is Bankrolling Ukraine Rebels: Ex-Separatist Official," Reuters, October 5, 2016.

Milton Keynes UK
Ingram Content Group UK Ltd.
UKHW050919100324
439022UK00006B/21